Mastering Email Security: A Comprehensive Guide to SPF, DKIM, and DMARC

Mastering Email Security: A Comprehensive Guide to SPF, DKIM, and DMARC

Whether you are just starting or looking to enhance your existing security measures, this guide will provide the knowledge and tools you need to protect against email-based threats effectively

Oleksandr Fisun

Copyright © 2025 Oleksandr Fisun
All rights reserved.
ISBN-13: 9798305149715

Dedication

To everyone I've encountered along the way who demonstrated the power of persistence and the value of honesty.

Table of Contents

CHAPTER 1: INTRODUCTION 1
    THE EVOLUTION OF EMAIL SECURITY 1
    THE RISE OF EMAIL THREATS 2
    TAKING SECURITY SERIOUSLY — THE BIRTH OF SPF, DKIM, AND DMARC ... 3
    WHY EMAIL AUTHENTICATION MATTERS TODAY 4
    ACTION STEPS 5

CHAPTER 2: UNDERSTANDING THE EMAIL THREAT LANDSCAPE 6
    INTRODUCTION TO THE THREAT LANDSCAPE 6
    COMMON EMAIL THREATS 6
    THE IMPACT OF EMAIL FRAUD 10
    EVOLVING TACTICS OF CYBERCRIMINALS 11
    THE IMPORTANCE OF PROACTIVE DEFENSE 12
    CONCLUSION 13
    ACTION STEPS 13

CHAPTER 3: SENDER POLICY FRAMEWORK (SPF) 14
    INTRODUCTION TO SPF 14
    UNDERSTANDING SPF 15
    HOW SPF WORKS 15
    SPF RECORD SYNTAX 17
    IMPLEMENTING SPF RECORDS 18
    BEST PRACTICES FOR SPF 19
    CHALLENGES AND LIMITATIONS OF SPF 20
    CONCLUSION 21
    CHECKLIST 21

CHAPTER 4: DOMAINKEYS IDENTIFIED MAIL (DKIM) 22
    INTRODUCTION TO DKIM 22
    WHAT IS DKIM? 23
    HOW DKIM WORKS 24
    DKIM-SIGNATURE HEADER 25
    SETTING UP DKIM 26
    BEST PRACTICES FOR DKIM 27
    CHALLENGES AND LIMITATIONS OF DKIM 28
    CONCLUSION 30
    CHECKLIST 30

CHAPTER 5: DOMAIN-BASED MESSAGE AUTHENTICATION, REPORTING & CONFORMANCE (DMARC) 31

Introduction to DMARC 31
What is DMARC? 32
How DMARC Works 33
Setting Up DMARC 34
Benefits of DMARC 36
Challenges and Best Practices for DMARC 38
Conclusion 39
Action Steps 39

CHAPTER 6: ALIGNING SPF, DKIM, AND DMARC FOR MAXIMUM EMAIL SECURITY 40

Introduction to Alignment 40
Importance of Alignment 40
Achieving Alignment: Practical Steps 42
Troubleshooting Common Alignment Issues 44
Best Practices for Maintaining Alignment 45
Conclusion 46
Checklist 47

CHAPTER 7: REAL-WORLD CASE STUDIES OF SPF, DKIM, AND DMARC IMPLEMENTATION 48

Introduction to Case Studies 48
Case Study 1: PayPal's Journey to Implement DMARC 48
Case Study 2: LinkedIn's Adoption of DKIM for Email Integrity 50
Case Study 3: Bank of America's Comprehensive Use of SPF, DKIM, and DMARC 51
Conclusion 53
Action Steps 53

CHAPTER 8: THE FUTURE OF EMAIL SECURITY 55

Introduction 55
Key Trends and Technologies in Email Security 55
What Organizations Can Do Today to Prepare for the Future 61
Conclusion 63
Action Steps 63

CHAPTER 9: INTEGRATING EMAIL SECURITY ADVANCEMENTS INTO YOUR INFRASTRUCTURE 64

Introduction 64
Understanding Your Current Position 64
Leveraging AI for Smarter Defense 65
Adopting Cloud-Based Email Security Solutions 65
Embrace the Zero Trust Model 66
Strengthening Email Authentication 66
Exploring Emerging Protocols 67
AI-Powered Threat Hunting and Automated Response 67
Fostering a Security-Aware Culture 68
Collaborate with Vendors and Partners 68

    Planning for Future Scalability and Threats 69
    Conclusion 69
    Checklist 70

CHAPTER 10: CONTINUOUS IMPROVEMENT AND FUTURE-PROOFING EMAIL SECURITY. 71

    Introduction 71
    Regular Assessments and Audits 71
    Adapting to Emerging Threats 72
    Employee Training and Awareness 72
    Embrace Automation for Efficiency 73
    Reviewing and Enhancing Policies 73
    Building a Resilient Incident Response Plan 73
    Partnering with Security Experts 74
    Future-Proofing with Emerging Technologies 74
    Encouraging a Culture of Continuous Improvement 74
    Conclusion 75
    Action Steps 75

GLOSSARY OF TERMS 76

RESOURCE LIST 84

Chapter 1: Introduction

The Evolution of Email Security

In the early 1970s, when computers filled entire rooms and only a handful of people had access to them, Ray Tomlinson was experimenting with ARPANET — the precursor to the Internet. With a three-meter network cable connecting two computers, he sent the very first email, marking the humble beginning of what would become a global phenomenon. This was when the '@' symbol was famously used to connect usernames to computer addresses, a practice we still use today.

> *Did you know?* That first email Ray Tomlinson sent was something incredibly mundane — most likely a random string of characters. He was simply testing how it worked, unaware that this small experiment would shape digital communication for decades to come.

By the 1990s, email was no longer just for computer engineers — it became mainstream. Families began getting email accounts, and businesses found it to be an indispensable tool for fast, cost-effective communication. It was like the digital version of sending a letter, but without the stamps or waiting days for a response. However, email was like an open house: anyone could knock on the door. The protocol (SMTP) used to send emails was designed with functionality in mind, not security. This oversight eventually led to a new problem — anyone could pretend to be someone else, which gave rise to a host of email-based threats.

As email continued to grow, it quickly became apparent that while it was a fantastic tool for communication, it was also vulnerable. The lack of built-in security features meant that cybercriminals had free rein to exploit it. Emails could be intercepted, altered, or used to impersonate others, and this open nature made it an easy target for malicious activity. The rapid adoption of email in both personal and professional spheres meant that these issues were affecting millions of users globally, and it became increasingly clear that something needed to change.

The Rise of Email Threats

As email spread around the world, so did the ways it could be exploited. Spam was like junk mail piling up in your mailbox, but unlike paper flyers, it cost nothing to send, which meant spammers could send it by the millions. These messages weren't just annoying; they were also a gateway to more dangerous threats.

More troubling were phishing attacks, where bad actors disguised themselves as legitimate organizations to trick people into sharing sensitive information like passwords and credit card numbers. Imagine opening your inbox to find an urgent email from your bank, complete with the logo and your name. It asks you to verify your account details due to a "security breach." This was the kind of well-crafted deception that started taking hold, leading many people to unwittingly hand over sensitive information to criminals.

It was a problem that grew bigger every year. Phishing attacks became more sophisticated, using personalized information to make messages convincing. Victims often suffered significant financial losses, and businesses faced damaged reputations.

> *Did you know?* The first recorded phishing attack was carried out in the mid-1990s, targeting America Online (AOL) users. Attackers created fake login screens to capture usernames and passwords, and it worked all too well.

Then came malware. Suddenly, emails weren't just nuisances — they were vehicles for malicious software that could do real damage. Remember the ILOVEYOU worm from 2000? It was an email that looked like a love letter. It seemed harmless, even charming — but as soon as people opened the attachment, it spread across networks, damaging files and wreaking havoc. It was a powerful reminder that even something seemingly innocent could be a threat.

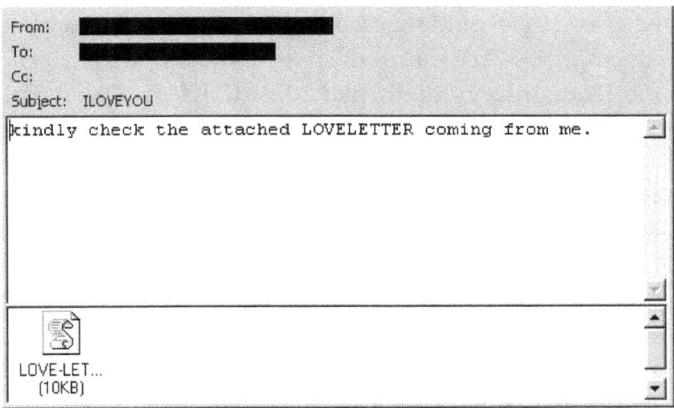

Figure 1: Email with an infected attachment

These threats made it clear that email desperately needed an upgrade in security. Malware could come in the form of attachments, links, or even seemingly harmless text, and once it infected a system, it could steal data, corrupt files, or hold entire networks hostage. The damage wasn't limited to individuals; entire organizations were brought to their knees by malware delivered via email.

In addition to phishing and malware, Business Email Compromise (BEC) started to emerge as a major threat. BEC attacks were particularly insidious because they often involved careful planning and research. Attackers would impersonate executives or trusted partners to trick employees into making wire transfers or sharing confidential information. Think of it like a master forger who spends time studying every detail of their target to perfectly impersonate someone important. These scams could lead to massive financial losses, sometimes reaching millions of dollars per incident.

Taking Security Seriously — The Birth of SPF, DKIM, and DMARC

To tackle these issues, the email community began to develop solutions, and thus, email authentication protocols like SPF, DKIM, and DMARC were born.

Sender Policy Framework (SPF) came first. It allowed domain owners to declare which servers were allowed to send emails on their behalf. Think of SPF as a bouncer at a club, checking the guest list to see who gets in. If you're on the list, you're allowed entry; if not, you're turned away. This simple but effective method allowed domain owners to say, "Only these servers are allowed to send emails for us." SPF was a significant step forward because it helped prevent unauthorized users from sending emails that appeared to come from legitimate domains, reducing the effectiveness of spam and phishing attacks.

Next came **DomainKeys Identified Mail (DKIM)**. DKIM is like sealing an envelope with a wax seal that only you have. When someone receives it, they can see that the seal hasn't been broken, meaning the content inside hasn't been tampered with. It's a way of saying, "This message is genuine and intact."

That's essentially what DKIM does. By using cryptographic authentication, DKIM ensures that the content of an email hasn't been altered during transit, providing both the sender and the recipient with greater confidence in the authenticity of the message.

Finally, **Domain-based Message Authentication, Reporting & Conformance (DMARC)** took things further by letting domain owners decide how to handle emails that failed SPF and DKIM verification – sort of like having security cameras at the party and deciding whether to let people in, throw them out, or just keep an eye on them. Plus, it provided valuable reports, so domain owners could see exactly who was trying to use their domain. This visibility allowed domain owners to identify and stop abuse of their domains, making DMARC a powerful tool in the fight against email fraud.

Did you know? DMARC's reporting feature is like having a security log that tells you who tried to get in, when, and why they were rejected. This feedback helps organizations and domain owners improve their security over time, fine-tuning their defenses based on real-world data.

Why Email Authentication Matters Today

In today's world, email security is more critical than ever. It isn't just about stopping spam; it's about protecting businesses, maintaining trust, and safeguarding personal information. Phishing emails and Business Email Compromise (BEC) attacks have become incredibly sophisticated, often costing companies millions of dollars in fraud and lost productivity. Imagine getting an email from your CEO asking for an urgent wire transfer. Without the right protections, it's easy for scammers to impersonate your boss, leading to huge financial losses, data breaches, and long-term reputational damage. Companies have lost millions because of email fraud, and recovery is often long and costly.

With email authentication protocols like SPF, DKIM, and DMARC, organizations can defend against many of these threats, ensuring their emails reach their intended recipients securely and building trust in their communications. Implementing these protocols means that legitimate emails are more likely to be delivered, while fraudulent ones are stopped before they can do harm. It's about creating a safer email ecosystem where both senders and recipients can feel confident.

Email authentication also enhances brand reputation. Customers are more likely to engage with emails they know are genuine, and they'll appreciate a brand that takes their privacy seriously. In a world full of cyber threats, trust is a competitive advantage.

Whether you're an IT professional, a business leader, or someone interested in making email safer, this guide will walk you through everything you need to know. We'll cover some technical steps, but also why they matter — because email security isn't just about stopping spam. It's about building a safer digital world for everyone.

Let's get started by exploring the email threat landscape in more detail in Chapter 2.

Action Steps

- **Reflect on Current State:** Consider how email is currently used within your organization and identify any potential vulnerabilities.
- **Set Goals:** Outline what you hope to achieve by improving your email security (e.g., reduce phishing incidents, improve brand reputation).
- **Preview What's Ahead:** Note any key chapters that seem most relevant to your organization's specific challenges.

Chapter 2: Understanding the Email Threat Landscape

Introduction to the Threat Landscape

It's a regular morning, and you open your email inbox. Among your usual messages, there's an email from your bank asking for urgent verification. It looks authentic, complete with logos and even your name. But there's a problem — it's not your bank. This kind of scenario plays out every day, highlighting just how vulnerable we all are when it comes to email security.

Email has become an integral part of our daily lives, both personally and professionally. We rely on it for everything from casual communication with friends to vital business transactions. But while email is incredibly convenient, its open nature also makes it one of the most exploited tools for cyberattacks. We've all had that moment of hesitation before clicking a link in an email — wondering if it's safe. This chapter will help you understand the threats behind that hesitation.

Common Email Threats

1. Phishing Attacks

Phishing is one of the most prevalent threats in the email landscape. In a phishing attack, cybercriminals send fraudulent emails that appear to come from a legitimate source — such as a trusted company, government entity, or even a known contact. These emails are designed to trick recipients into taking actions that compromise their sensitive information, such as clicking malicious links, downloading harmful attachments, or revealing login credentials.

For instance, in 2016, a spear-phishing attack tricked employees into handing over their credentials, leading to the infamous Democratic National Committee breach. Such incidents demonstrate how sophisticated and damaging phishing can be.

Phishing can take many forms:

- **Deceptive Phishing**: Think of an email saying, "Your account will be locked in 24 hours unless you click this link." It's generic but relies on creating fear and urgency to force quick action.

- **Spear Phishing**: These attacks are more targeted, using personal information to make the email appear more legitimate. Attackers often research their victims on social media to customize their approach and add a personal touch.

- **Whaling**: A specialized form of spear phishing that targets high-profile individuals, such as executives or senior managers. Picture an attacker going after a company's CFO, using information about an upcoming merger to add credibility. This type of attack can have catastrophic consequences.

The most concerning aspect of phishing attacks is their ability to bypass traditional security measures, especially when they are well-crafted. Cybercriminals know how to leverage emotions—fear, urgency, or curiosity—to manipulate recipients into acting quickly without considering the risks.

2. Business Email Compromise (BEC)

Business Email Compromise (BEC) is a more sophisticated and targeted threat. In a BEC attack, cybercriminals impersonate a trusted party—often a company executive or a business partner—to deceive employees into making wire transfers or sharing sensitive company information. BEC attacks typically involve extensive research, where the attacker studies the organization's communication habits and hierarchical structure to make their impersonation convincing.

Picture this: The finance department receives an email from the CEO while they're traveling. The email asks for an urgent wire transfer to a new vendor. It appears legitimate — the attacker has even included details about the CEO's recent meeting. Under pressure, the employee completes the transfer, unaware that they've just fallen for a well-planned BEC scam.

> *Did you know?* According to the FBI, BEC scams have caused over $55 billion[1] in losses worldwide since 2013. It's a reminder that even one successful impersonation can lead to massive financial fallout.

BEC attacks have been highly successful, primarily because they exploit trust, urgency, and authority such as "The CEO needs this done immediately while traveling," making employees feel they must act without question. Unlike mass phishing, which relies on casting a wide net, BEC attacks are strategic, with attackers often spending weeks or even months preparing for their move.

3. Malware Distribution

Malware delivered via email is another significant threat. Cybercriminals often use malicious attachments or links to infect victims' systems with viruses, ransomware, and other harmful software. These emails might appear to be something important—like an invoice, a job application, or a shipping notification—tempting recipients to click without thinking twice.

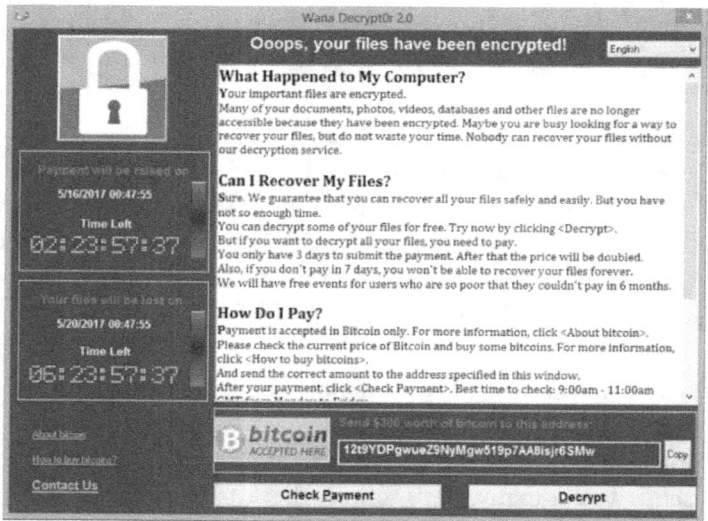

Figure 2: Screenshot of the ransom note left on an infected system

---

[1] https://www.ic3.gov/PSA/2024/PSA240911

A notable example of ransomware that shook the world in 2017 was WannaCry. While it exploited a known operating system vulnerability to spread rapidly across networks, many initial infections originated from phishing emails. Once a user inadvertently opened an infected attachment or clicked a compromised link, WannaCry encrypted their files and demanded payment to restore access. Its impact was felt across the globe, disrupting hospitals, businesses, and critical infrastructure. This event served as a stark reminder that one careless click can lead to devastating consequences.

> *Did you know?* WannaCry infected more than 200,000 machines in over 150 countries within just a few days. Even organizations with sophisticated IT systems struggled to contain it, underscoring that vigilance and proper email security measures are essential for everyone—no matter their size or sector.

4. Spam and Unsolicited Emails

Spam, although often seen as a mere annoyance, can also pose serious risks. Spam emails flood inboxes, making it challenging for recipients to discern legitimate messages from junk. Think of an employee spending several minutes each day clearing spam. Over a year, those minutes add up to hours of lost productivity — just because of unsolicited emails.

> *Did you know?* It's estimated that 85% of all email traffic is spam. Without proper filtering, organizations would struggle to find legitimate communication amidst all the noise.

Beyond cluttering inboxes, spam is frequently used as a delivery method for phishing links and malware – sometimes, one careless click can bring down an entire network, leading to significant operational disruption.

For businesses, managing spam and ensuring that employees do not fall victim to malicious spam emails requires strong spam filtering technologies and user education.

To protect against common email threats, users can verify URLs before clicking, hover over links to check their authenticity, and confirm requests for sensitive information via alternate channels (e.g., calling the bank's official number).

The Impact of Email Fraud

The impact of email-based threats goes far beyond the inconvenience of a full spam folder. Falling for a phishing scam can feel like having your personal space violated. Not only might you lose money, but your sense of security can be deeply shaken.

1. Financial Losses

Many email attacks are motivated by financial gain, and the costs can be enormous. Falling for a phishing or BEC scam can feel like your house being burglarized — not only is there financial loss, but also a deep sense of violation. The damage often goes beyond money; it affects people's sense of security and trust.

Ransomware delivered through email can also have dire financial consequences, with attackers demanding payments in exchange for the decryption of company data. Even when victims refuse to pay, the cost of recovery, including downtime and data restoration, can be substantial.

2. Data Breaches

Email attacks can lead to significant data breaches, where sensitive company information, customer data, or employee records are exposed. Imagine that a phishing email gives attackers access to your company's database, leaking sensitive employee information. Now, every employee has to worry about identity theft — all because of one email.

Such breaches often result in regulatory penalties, lawsuits, and damage to customer trust. In the 2016 Democratic National Committee (DNC) breach[2], attackers used a phishing email that tricked a key individual into entering their credentials on a fake login page. The result was a massive leak of confidential emails that changed the course of political events.

3. Reputational Damage

When an organization suffers an email breach, its reputation is often one of the first casualties. Customers and business partners expect companies to protect their data. When that trust is broken, it can be challenging to rebuild. The negative publicity and loss of customer confidence can lead to a long-term decline in brand

---

[2] https://en.wikipedia.org/wiki/2016_Democratic_National_Committee_email_leak

value and market position.

Evolving Tactics of Cybercriminals

Cybercriminals are constantly adapting their tactics to stay ahead of security measures. Today's email threats are more sophisticated than ever, employing new techniques and technologies to evade detection.

1. Social Engineering

Social engineering is a core component of many email-based attacks. Cybercriminals manipulate human psychology to achieve their goals, using tactics like:

- **Pretexting**: Imagine getting a call from "IT support" claiming they need your login details to resolve a critical issue. Attackers use pretexting to establish legitimacy and gain access.

- **Baiting**: An employee sees a USB drive labelled "Bonus Documents" left in the breakroom. The curiosity leads them to plug it into their computer, not knowing it's filled with malware.

- **Impersonation**: One attacker posed as a company's vendor and requested a payment update. The accountant, thinking it was legitimate, made the transfer — directly into the attacker's hands.

Attackers use information gathered from social media and other public sources to make their emails highly convincing. Personal touches — like referring to the recipient by name or mentioning a recent event — can make the difference between a successful attack and an ignored email.

2. Exploitation of Emerging Technologies

Cybercriminals are also exploiting emerging technologies to enhance the effectiveness of their attacks. Artificial Intelligence (AI) and machine learning are being used to craft more believable phishing emails, automate attacks at scale, and identify vulnerable targets. Attackers are using AI to mimic writing styles, making phishing emails almost indistinguishable from legitimate ones. Imagine getting a deepfake voicemail from your boss, urging you to approve a payment — it's an unsettling new reality.

The Importance of Proactive Defense

To stay ahead of cybercriminals, organizations must take a proactive approach to email security. Imagine if every employee in your organization felt confident enough to recognize phishing attempts and report them. With a combination of strong email authentication protocols (SPF, DKIM, DMARC) and a well-informed team, organizations can transform email from a potential vulnerability into a secure, trusted communication channel.

1. Email Authentication Protocols

Email authentication protocols like SPF, DKIM, and DMARC are essential tools for verifying sender identity and preventing email spoofing. By implementing these protocols, organizations can significantly reduce the risk of fraudulent emails being delivered to users' inboxes.

- **SPF (Sender Policy Framework)**: Helps identify which mail servers are authorized to send emails on behalf of a domain.

- **DKIM (DomainKeys Identified Mail)**: Uses digital signatures to verify that an email was not altered during transit and that it originated from an authorized domain.

- **DMARC (Domain-based Message Authentication, Reporting, and Conformance)**: Builds on SPF and DKIM to provide domain owners with greater control over email authentication and reporting, allowing them to define policies for handling unauthenticated messages.

2. User Education

Technology alone is not enough. Cybercriminals often target the weakest link in the security chain—the user. Training employees isn't just about showing them slides; it's about engaging them with real-life simulations. Picture a training exercise where employees are sent fake phishing emails, and those who identify the threats receive small rewards. This kind of interactive training can go a long way in keeping your organization secure.

3. Incident Response Planning

Even with the best defenses in place, incidents can happen. Having a well-defined incident response plan ensures that organizations can quickly respond to email attacks, contain damage, and restore normal operations. Incident response should involve cross-functional teams, including IT, legal, communications, and management, to handle all aspects of the response effectively.

Conclusion

The email threat landscape is constantly evolving, with cybercriminals finding new ways to exploit vulnerabilities and bypass security measures. Phishing, Business Email Compromise, malware distribution, and spam are just a few of the many threats that target email users daily. Knowledge is power. By understanding these threats, you are already taking the first step toward making your email environment safer for everyone.

By implementing a combination of technical solutions, such as SPF, DKIM, and DMARC, along with user education and proactive incident response planning, organizations can protect themselves against the pervasive threats lurking in the email ecosystem. In the next chapter, we'll take a closer look at how the Sender Policy Framework (SPF) works and how implementing it can be the first solid step toward fortifying your domain's email security.

Action Steps

- **Identify Common Threats:** List the email threats most relevant to your organization (phishing, BEC, malware, spam).
- **Assess Current Controls:** Check if your current tools and training address these threats.
- **Plan User Education:** Consider scheduling a security awareness session or phishing simulation to improve staff vigilance.

Chapter 3: Sender Policy Framework (SPF)

Introduction to SPF

Imagine sending an invitation for an exclusive event — only the people you personally authorize should be able to attend. But without a guest list, anyone could show up and pretend they belong. SPF works in a similar way: it creates a "guest list" of authorized email servers that can send emails on behalf of your domain. This helps prevent impersonators from hijacking your brand, giving you better control over who gets to "speak" in your name.

Email spoofing and unauthorized use of domains have been significant challenges in email security since its inception. The Sender Policy Framework (SPF) was developed to address these issues and is one of the foundational email authentication protocols designed to help domain owners regain control over who is allowed to send emails on their behalf. If the email originates from an authorized server, it is more likely to be accepted as legitimate. If it comes from an unauthorized source, the recipient server may reject it or flag it as suspicious.

SPF plays a crucial role in establishing trust between email senders and recipients. Without it, malicious actors could easily impersonate legitimate domains, causing users to fall victim to scams, malware, and other cyber threats. SPF helps reduce the effectiveness of these attacks and serves as a critical building block for a more secure email ecosystem.

Understanding SPF

What is SPF?

SPF stands for Sender Policy Framework. It's a simple yet powerful way for domain owners to prevent email spoofing. By publishing an SPF record, domain owners can state explicitly which IP addresses are authorized to send emails for their domain. This enables recipient mail servers to verify that incoming messages are genuinely from the domain they claim to be from.

SPF works by leveraging DNS TXT records to store authorized IP addresses. These records are then referenced whenever an email claiming to be from the domain is received. By comparing the sender's IP address with the list of authorized senders, the recipient server can verify if the email is authentic.

The implementation of SPF has helped significantly in reducing spam and phishing attacks that rely on forging sender addresses. While it isn't foolproof, when used alongside other email authentication methods like DKIM and DMARC, it provides an effective line of defense against email-based attacks. The importance of SPF lies in its ability to prevent unauthorized users from impersonating trusted domains, thereby mitigating the risk of fraud and protecting both businesses and their customers.

How SPF Works

To better understand SPF, let's break down its workflow into a series of steps:

1. **Email Transmission**: When someone sends an email, their mail server (called the Mail Transfer Agent or MTA) sends the email, which includes information such as the sender's domain.

2. **Recipient's SPF Check**: When the recipient's server receives the email, it identifies the domain specified in the "Return-Path" field of the email header.

3. **DNS Query for SPF Record**: The recipient server queries the DNS for the SPF record of the sender's domain. The SPF record contains a list of IP addresses and mechanisms authorized to send emails for that domain.

4. **Validation**: The recipient server compares the sender's IP address to the

IPs listed in the SPF record.
   a. If the sender's IP matches an authorized IP, the SPF check "passes," and the email is more likely to be accepted.
   b. If the IP doesn't match, the SPF check "fails," and the recipient server can reject the email or flag it as potentially fraudulent.
5. **Handling the Result**: The SPF record also includes a directive (usually -all, ~all, or +all) that tells the receiving server what to do if the email fails validation.

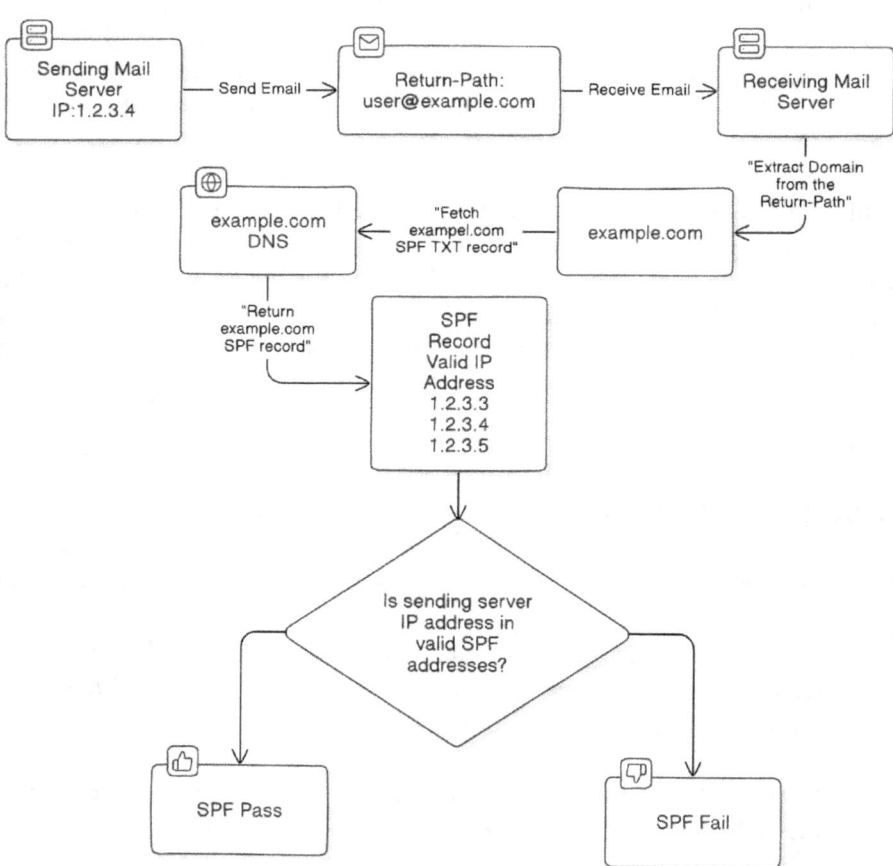

Figure 3: How SPF Works

The outcome of an SPF check directly impacts how an email is processed. A "pass" result indicates that the email is coming from a legitimate source, increasing its chances of being delivered to the recipient's inbox. On the other hand, a "fail" result can lead to the email being blocked, sent to the spam folder, or tagged as suspicious. The flexibility of SPF allows domain owners to define how strict or lenient they want to be when dealing with unauthorized senders, providing a customizable approach to email security.

SPF Record Syntax

An SPF record is published in a DNS TXT record. Here's a breakdown of the key components of a typical SPF record:

- **v=spf1**: Indicates the SPF version (currently always v=spf1).

- **Mechanisms**: Specifies the rules for how to handle the sender's IP address. Examples of mechanisms include:

    - **ip4** and **ip6**: Specify the IP addresses or ranges allowed to send emails. For example, ip4:203.0.113.0/24 means any address in that range is authorized.

    - **a**: Authorizes the IPs specified by the A record of the domain.

    - **mx**: Authorizes the IPs associated with the domain's MX (Mail Exchange) records.

    - **include**: Refers to another domain's SPF record that is also authorized to send emails for your domain. This is useful when third-party services are used to send emails on behalf of your domain.

    - **all**: Matches any address not previously matched by other mechanisms and is typically used to define what happens if no other rules match.

Each mechanism plays a specific role in determining which servers are allowed to send emails for a domain. For example, using the **mx** mechanism allows any mail server listed in your domain's MX records to be authorized. The **include** mechanism is particularly important when using third-party services, as it allows you to delegate authority to another domain's SPF policy, ensuring those services can send emails without causing SPF checks to fail.

Here's an example of a basic SPF record:

```
v=spf1 ip4:203.0.113.0/24 include:_spf.thirdparty.com -all
```

This means emails are allowed from the IP range 203.0.113.0 to 203.0.113.255, and IP addresses from service thirdparty.com. All others should be rejected.

- **v=spf1**: Version of SPF.

- **ip4:203.0.113.0/24**: Authorizes emails from any address in this IP range.

- **include:_spf.thirdparty.com**: Allows emails from a third-party service.

- **-all**: Indicates a "hard fail," meaning emails from unauthorized IPs should be rejected.

Did you know? Using the `-all` directive enforces a "hard fail," which means emails from unauthorized IPs are outright rejected. This strict policy provides strong security but requires careful planning. During the initial implementation phase, it's a good idea to use `~all` ("soft fail") to monitor potential issues before switching to `-all` for full protection.

Implementing SPF Records

Implementing SPF for your domain involves a few straightforward steps:

1. **Identify Your Sending Sources**: Make a list of all servers and services that send emails on behalf of your domain. This includes your company's internal mail servers, any cloud services, third-party email marketing platforms, and other tools. Accurately identifying all your sending sources is crucial for creating an effective SPF record.

2. **Create the SPF Record**: Construct an SPF record that includes all authorized senders. Use mechanisms such as `ip4`, `mx`, and `include` to define who is allowed to send emails. Be comprehensive but concise, as

SPF records must comply with the 10-DNS-lookup limit.

3. **Publish the SPF Record**: Publish your SPF record as a DNS TXT record for your domain. You'll need access to your DNS management console to add or edit this record. Ensure that the SPF record is correctly formatted and free of syntax errors, as even minor mistakes can cause SPF checks to fail.

4. **Test and Validate**: Once your SPF record is published, it's important to test it. There are various online tools that can validate SPF records to ensure they are correctly formatted and working as expected. Testing helps identify any issues before they affect email delivery.

Imagine building a house but skipping the inspection — small errors could lead to major problems later. Testing your SPF record is similar. By validating your SPF setup, you're ensuring that all authorized sources are accounted for, and everything is working as expected. Tools like **MXToolbox**[3] can help ensure your SPF record is correct before it affects your email deliverability.

Best Practices for SPF

- **Keep Your Record Updated**: Regularly update your SPF record to reflect any changes in your sending infrastructure. Adding new servers or services? Make sure they're included in your SPF record. Removing outdated entries can help avoid unnecessary DNS lookups and potential errors.

- **Minimize DNS Lookups**: SPF records have a limit of 10 DNS lookups. If you exceed this limit, the SPF check will fail. Use tools to flatten your SPF record if it becomes too complex. Flattening involves replacing includes with the corresponding IP addresses to reduce the number of lookups, ensuring compliance with the SPF specification.

- **Use -all Directive**: Initially, you may use ~all (soft fail) while testing your configuration, but it's best to switch to -all (hard fail) once you're confident in your setup. This ensures that unauthorized emails are outright rejected, providing stronger protection against spoofing.

---

[3] https://mxtoolbox.com/SPFRecordGenerator.aspx

- **Monitor SPF Results**: Monitoring your SPF results is like keeping an eye on your home security cameras. You get to see who tried to "get in" and whether they were authorized. DMARC reports serve as your security footage, giving you insights into any unauthorized activities that may need addressing.

- **Use Short TTL Values During Testing**: When first implementing or making significant changes to your SPF record, use short Time-to-Live (TTL) values for your DNS record. This allows for quicker propagation and makes it easier to correct errors without waiting for long cache times to expire.

Challenges and Limitations of SPF

While SPF is a valuable tool in the fight against email spoofing, it has its limitations:

- **Forwarding Issues**: If an email is forwarded, the original sender's IP address may not align with the authorized IPs in the SPF record, causing the SPF check to fail.

> *Did you know?* One of the reasons forwarding is such a challenge for SPF is that when an email is forwarded, the new server's IP address isn't in the original SPF record. Using DKIM alongside SPF can help solve this problem because DKIM ensures the email's content hasn't changed, even if the IP address is different.

- **DNS Lookup Limit**: The 10-lookup limit can be a challenge for larger organizations that use multiple third-party services. When the limit is exceeded, SPF validation fails, which can lead to legitimate emails being flagged as spam. Using services like SPF flattening tools can help mitigate this issue by reducing the number of DNS lookups.

- **Lack of Encryption**: SPF only authenticates the server sending the email; it does not encrypt the message content or verify the integrity of the message body. This means that while SPF can confirm whether an email is coming from an authorized server, it cannot guarantee that the message content hasn't been tampered with during transit.

- **Dependency on DNS Availability**: Since SPF relies on DNS records, any downtime or issues with DNS can disrupt SPF verification. Ensuring high availability and redundancy for DNS services is critical to maintaining effective SPF functionality.

Conclusion

SPF is a foundational component of email security that helps reduce the risk of domain spoofing and phishing attacks. By allowing domain owners to publish a list of authorized email senders, SPF gives organizations more control over their email reputation and helps recipients verify the legitimacy of incoming messages. Although it has its challenges, SPF is most effective when combined with DKIM and DMARC, creating a layered defense against email-based threats.

While SPF might seem daunting at first, it's all about establishing clear rules for who can "speak" on behalf of your domain. By following best practices, staying vigilant, and leveraging tools to monitor and update your SPF record, you can significantly improve your email security posture. Remember, email security is a journey, and SPF is one of the critical steps to keep your organization safe.

In the next chapter, we will explore **DomainKeys Identified Mail (DKIM)**, another key protocol that works alongside SPF to ensure the integrity and authenticity of email communications. DKIM provides a way to digitally sign email messages, making it an essential tool for preventing tampering and ensuring that emails reach their intended recipients without compromise.

Checklist

[ ] Identify all servers and services sending email on behalf of your domain.
[ ] Create or update your SPF record with authorized IPs and domains.
[ ] Validate your SPF record using online tools (e.g., MXToolbox).
[ ] Set a reminder to revisit and update your SPF record regularly (e.g., every 6 months).

Chapter 4: DomainKeys Identified Mail (DKIM)

Introduction to DKIM

Imagine you're sending a package to a friend, and you seal it with a unique wax stamp that only you have. If the package arrives and the seal is intact, your friend knows it hasn't been tampered with and is truly from you. DKIM works similarly for email — it adds a digital "seal" that ensures messages are not altered during their journey across the internet.

In a world where email security is constantly under threat, DomainKeys Identified Mail (DKIM) plays a vital role in authenticating email messages and maintaining trust between senders and recipients. While SPF ensures that emails

Figure 4: Traditional wax seal used to authenticate the sender of a letter, akin to how DKIM verifies email authenticity with a digital stamp

are coming from authorized servers, DKIM goes a step further by verifying that the content of an email has not been altered during transit. This is achieved through cryptographic signatures that help establish the authenticity of the message and reassure recipients that the email truly comes from the domain it claims to be from.

DKIM is like the wax seal of the digital world — when an email leaves its originating server, it is stamped with a signature that cannot be altered without breaking the seal. When the email arrives at its destination, the receiving server checks this signature to ensure that the email is exactly as it was when it left the sender. By doing so, DKIM helps combat a wide range of email-based attacks, including phishing, email tampering, and other forms of impersonation.

Without DKIM, there is no reliable way for recipients to know whether the content of an email has been altered along the way. Attackers could easily modify emails during transit, inserting malicious links or altering attachments, thereby compromising the security of the recipient. DKIM helps to prevent such malicious activity, making it an essential component of email security.

What is DKIM?

DomainKeys Identified Mail (DKIM) is an email authentication protocol that allows domain owners to attach a digital signature to their outgoing emails. This signature, created with cryptographic keys, is used by the recipient's server to verify that the email has not been altered and that it is truly from the claimed domain.

The goal of DKIM is to maintain the integrity and authenticity of email messages. While SPF helps verify the identity of the server sending the message, DKIM ensures that the message content itself has not been modified. Together, they provide a stronger defense against various forms of email fraud, such as spoofing, phishing, and man-in-the-middle attacks.

When an email is sent, DKIM uses a private key to generate a unique digital signature for the message. The recipient server then retrieves the corresponding public key, which is published in the sender domain's DNS records, to validate the signature. If the signature matches, the email is considered authentic and unaltered. This verification process not only confirms that the email is genuine but also provides confidence that the email content has not been tampered with during its journey across the internet.

How DKIM Works

The process of DKIM can be broken down into the following steps:

1. **Signing the Email**: Picture the private key as a unique signature stamp that belongs solely to the domain owner. When an email is sent, the outgoing mail server uses a private key to generate a digital signature. This signature is based on certain components of the email, such as the subject line, headers, and body content, to ensure that even minor changes

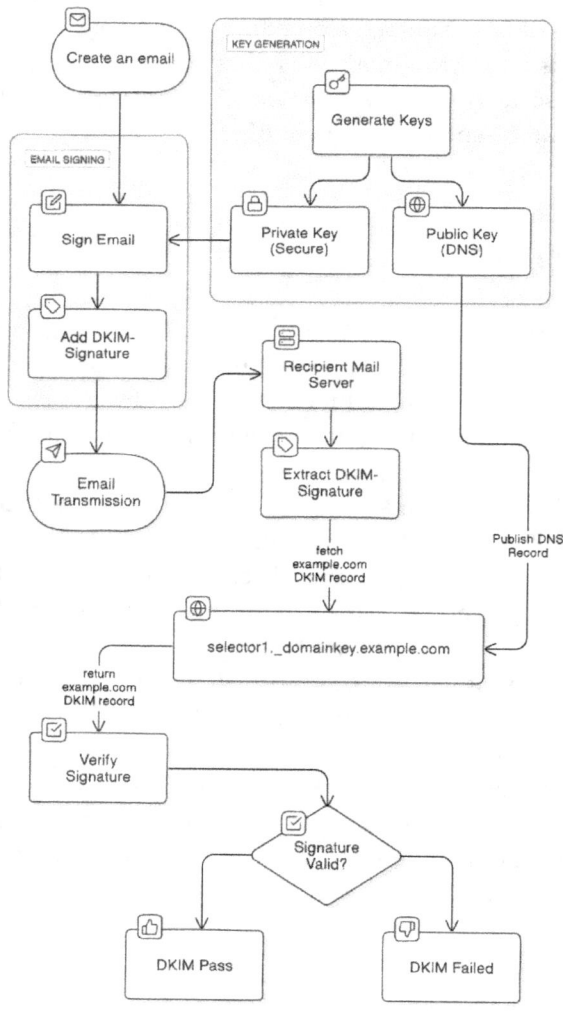

Figure 5: How DKIM Works

to the message would invalidate the signature. The signature is then added to the email header as a field called "DKIM-Signature."

2. **Publishing the Public Key**: The public key is like a matching stamp verifier. By publishing it in the domain's DNS records, the recipient's server can look it up and confirm that the signature on the email is genuine, ensuring its authenticity. The DNS record that contains the public key is called a DKIM record and is associated with a specific selector to differentiate between different signing keys.

3. **Verifying the Signature**: Think of the recipient's server as the inspector — using the public key to validate that the stamp is legitimate. When the recipient's mail server receives the email, it retrieves the public key from the sender's DNS records. The server then uses this key to verify the DKIM signature. If the signature matches, it confirms that the email has not been altered and that it genuinely comes from the domain it claims to be from. If the signature fails verification, the email may be flagged as suspicious, rejected, or marked as spam, depending on the recipient's email security policy.

DKIM-Signature Header

The DKIM signature is added to the email as a header called **DKIM-Signature**. This header contains several components that help the recipient server verify the message:

- **v**: Version of DKIM being used (currently always `v=1`).

- **a**: The signing algorithm used (typically `RSA-SHA256`).

- **d**: The domain that signed the message.

- **s**: The selector, which helps identify the correct public key to use for verification.

- **bh**: The hash of the body of the email, ensuring that the content has not been altered.

- **b**: The actual digital signature generated by the private key.

Each component of the DKIM-Signature header plays a crucial role in the verification process. The **selector** (s) is particularly important, as it points the recipient server to the appropriate DNS record containing the public key. This allows organizations to use multiple keys for different purposes or to rotate keys as needed without affecting the entire email infrastructure.

An example of a DKIM signature header might look like this:

```
DKIM-Signature: v=1; a=rsa-sha256; d=example.com; s=selector;
bh=7l9vsm1J26L5oz8cR/5rGz4j4Nm7GF4Z+Kx2CQ==;
b=YI9OFRJ/Ev5kwQlj8R4t2gUjSp3G9P/f9Ic6OjWcXs3HhNLN9==
```

In this example:

- **v=1**: Specifies the version of DKIM.

- **a=rsa-sha256**: Indicates the signing algorithm used to generate the signature.

- **d=example.com**: Shows the domain that signed the email.

- **s=selector**: Refers to the DNS record where the public key is stored.

- **bh**: Provides the hash value of the body content, ensuring the content hasn't changed.

- **b**: Represents the unique signature generated for this email.

> *Did you know?* The **hash value** (bh) in the DKIM-Signature header ensures the message's integrity. Even a small change—like an added space or altered punctuation—would result in a completely different hash, invalidating the signature. This is why DKIM is effective at detecting even the slightest tampering.

Setting Up DKIM

Implementing DKIM involves a few key steps, which can be broken down as follows:

1. **Generate DKIM Keys**: To start, you need to generate a pair of cryptographic keys — a private key and a public key. The private key is

used to sign outgoing emails, while the public key will be published in your DNS records. Many email service providers offer tools to easily generate DKIM keys, providing you with only the public key while keeping the private key secure.

2. **Publish the Public Key**: The public key must be published in your DNS records as a TXT record. The DNS record will include the selector used to identify the key and the domain it is associated with. The selector is important because it allows you to use multiple DKIM keys and rotate them without affecting other parts of your email infrastructure.

3. **Configure Your Mail Server**: Once the keys are generated and the public key is published, configure your mail server to sign all outgoing emails with the private key. Most modern mail servers, such as Microsoft Exchange, Postfix, and Gmail, support DKIM signing. Proper configuration ensures that every outgoing email is signed, providing consistent security across all messages.

4. **Test and Validate**: After DKIM is set up, it is important to test and validate the configuration. There are several online tools available that can check whether your DKIM implementation is functioning correctly, allowing you to verify that your emails are being signed and that the signatures are valid. Testing also helps identify any issues, such as incorrect DNS entries or misconfigured mail server settings, before they can affect email deliverability.

Validation should be an ongoing process, particularly after making changes to your DNS records or email infrastructure. Periodically testing DKIM helps ensure that everything continues to work as expected, and that your email security is not inadvertently compromised.

Best Practices for DKIM

- **Use Strong Keys**: It's important to use strong cryptographic keys to sign your emails. A key length of at least 2048 bits is recommended to provide adequate security. Keys that are too short may be vulnerable to attacks, allowing cybercriminals to forge signatures and potentially impersonate your domain.

- **Rotate Keys Regularly**: To enhance security, you should periodically rotate your DKIM keys. This involves generating new private and public keys and updating your DNS records. Key rotation helps minimize the impact of a key compromise, reducing the risk that an attacker could use a compromised key to send fraudulent emails. Best practice is to rotate DKIM keys at least once a year or more frequently if you handle highly sensitive communications. For example, if you initially use the selector 'selector2024,' create a new selector like 'selector2025' when you rotate keys next year. Update your DNS and mail server configurations accordingly, test thoroughly, then retire the old key.

- **Monitor DKIM Results**: Implement DMARC to receive reports on the results of DKIM checks. These reports provide valuable insight into whether your emails are being properly authenticated and can help you identify any unauthorized use of your domain. Monitoring these reports allows you to take proactive measures to address any issues before they escalate.

- **Use Appropriate Selector Names**: When generating DKIM keys, use meaningful selector names that make it easy to manage and rotate keys. For example, using names like "selector2024" helps indicate when the key was created and makes it easier to keep track of key rotations. Using descriptive selectors can simplify the process of updating and managing DKIM keys.

- **Ensure DNS Availability**: Since DKIM relies on DNS to publish the public key, it is critical to ensure that your DNS servers are highly available and redundant. Any downtime could result in emails failing DKIM verification, affecting email deliverability. Implementing redundant DNS infrastructure and monitoring DNS availability are crucial steps in maintaining reliable DKIM functionality.

Challenges and Limitations of DKIM

While DKIM is a powerful tool for ensuring the integrity and authenticity of email messages, it is not without its limitations:

- **Complex Setup**: Setting up DKIM can be more complex than SPF, requiring the generation and management of cryptographic keys, as well as modifications to DNS records. For smaller organizations, this complexity may be a barrier to adoption, especially if they lack the technical expertise or resources to implement DKIM effectively. However, many cloud-based email providers like Google Workspace, Microsoft 365, and Proton Mail simplify this process by generating DKIM keys automatically and guiding users through the setup process, significantly reducing the technical burden.

- **No Protection Against Replay Attacks**: DKIM does not inherently protect against replay attacks, where a malicious actor captures a signed email and sends it again to multiple recipients. The signature remains valid, making it appear as though the email is legitimate.

> *Did you know?* While DKIM does not inherently protect against replay attacks, combining it with SPF and DMARC policies greatly reduces the risk. DMARC adds an extra layer of scrutiny, allowing domain owners to specify exactly how to handle unauthorized emails, minimizing the damage that replay attacks can cause.

- **Dependency on DNS**: DKIM's reliance on DNS makes it crucial to ensure high availability and accuracy of DNS records. Using trusted DNS management providers like GoDaddy, Cloudflare or AWS Route 53 can help minimize outages and misconfigurations. These providers also offer monitoring services to alert you if there are any issues, ensuring that DKIM verification remains reliable.

- **Not End-to-End Encryption**: DKIM ensures that an email is legitimate and unaltered, but it does not encrypt the email content. This means that while DKIM can verify that an email is authentic, the content is still visible to anyone who can intercept the message during transit. To protect content confidentiality, additional encryption methods like Transport Layer Security (TLS) should be used. Combining DKIM with other encryption methods ensures both authenticity and privacy.

- **Complex Key Management**: The management of cryptographic keys can be challenging, especially for large organizations that send a high volume of emails or use multiple domains. Key rotation, selector management, and DNS updates require careful planning and execution to avoid disruptions in email delivery or security lapses. Organizations with on-premises email infrastructure should have clear policies and procedures for key management to mitigate these challenges. However, cloud-based email providers often handle key management automatically, including key generation, rotation, and updates. This makes it much easier for organizations to maintain strong DKIM security without the need for extensive manual intervention.

Conclusion

DKIM is a powerful email authentication tool that adds a layer of trust to digital communication. By attaching a unique signature to outgoing messages, it allows the recipient to verify that the message is genuine and hasn't been modified. Think of it as a digital guarantee — ensuring that the email really is from who it says it is and that nobody altered it during its journey. When used alongside SPF and DMARC, DKIM creates a robust framework for combating email-based attacks and maintaining trust in email communications.

While DKIM does have its challenges, many of these can be mitigated with the help of modern cloud email providers. These platforms provide tools and automation that simplify DKIM setup and management, making it easier for organizations of all sizes to implement and benefit from DKIM without needing extensive technical expertise. By adopting DKIM, organizations and domain owners can significantly improve their email security posture, reduce the risk of domain spoofing, and enhance trust in their communications.

In the next chapter, we will discuss **Domain-based Message Authentication, Reporting & Conformance (DMARC)**, the protocol that ties SPF and DKIM together and provides domain owners with greater control over email authentication, along with valuable reporting insights. DMARC is a critical tool for any organization looking to protect its domain from abuse and ensure that its email communications are secure.

Checklist

[ ] Generate and publish DKIM keys (use at least 2048-bit keys).
[ ] Configure your mail server to sign all outgoing mail.
[ ] Test and validate DKIM signatures with online tools.
[ ] Plan for periodic key rotation (annually or bi-annually).

Chapter 5: Domain-based Message Authentication, Reporting & Conformance (DMARC)

Introduction to DMARC

Picture this: you run a business, and suddenly someone out there is impersonating your brand, sending emails to your customers pretending to be you. Not only does this damage your reputation, but it also puts your customers at risk.

Spoofing, phishing, and other forms of email fraud have become increasingly sophisticated, making email security more challenging. This is where Domain-based Message Authentication, Reporting & Conformance (DMARC) comes into play. DMARC is an essential email authentication protocol that builds upon SPF and DKIM to give domain owners more control over their email security, protect their domains from abuse, and provide greater transparency through reporting.

DMARC provides a critical link between SPF, DKIM, and the recipient's email server, allowing domain owners to specify what should happen if an email fails authentication checks. This means that domain owners can instruct email servers to quarantine, reject, or allow messages that fail to authenticate. Additionally, DMARC generates valuable reports, which provide insight into the sources of email traffic, enabling domain owners to monitor and address unauthorized use of their domain. These reports help organizations build a stronger understanding of how their domain is being used, both legitimately and illegitimately, which ultimately helps in refining email security practices. By using DMARC, domain owners can take proactive steps to mitigate threats and improve their email ecosystem's overall integrity and reliability.

What is DMARC?

Domain-based Message Authentication, Reporting & Conformance (DMARC) is an email authentication protocol that helps protect domains from being used for email spoofing, phishing, and other types of cyberattacks. It works by aligning the results of SPF and DKIM with the domain in the "From" header of an email. DMARC allows domain owners to set a policy that specifies how to handle emails that fail these authentication checks, giving them more control over their email traffic.

DMARC effectively combines the strengths of SPF and DKIM, acting as a referee between these two protocols and the recipient's server. It's like having a final checkpoint to determine whether an email should pass, be questioned, or blocked outright.

DMARC is designed to solve the problem of unauthenticated emails reaching recipients and causing harm, such as data breaches, financial loss, and brand damage. By implementing DMARC, domain owners can not only reduce the chances of their domains being used in fraudulent emails but also increase the trustworthiness of their communications. This increased trust helps strengthen relationships with customers, partners, and other stakeholders who rely on email as a primary form of communication. Furthermore, by enforcing DMARC policies, domain owners can ensure that only legitimate emails from trusted sources are delivered to recipients' inboxes, thereby reducing the likelihood of successful phishing attacks.

DMARC policies are defined in DNS TXT records, similar to SPF and DKIM, and can specify actions such as:

- **None**: No specific action is taken if an email fails authentication, but reports are generated for monitoring.

- **Quarantine**: Emails that fail DMARC checks are marked as suspicious and sent to the recipient's spam or junk folder.

- **Reject**: Emails that fail DMARC checks are rejected outright, preventing them from being delivered.

By choosing the appropriate policy, domain owners can strike the right balance between ensuring security and maintaining email deliverability.

> *Did you know?* Starting with a "none" policy is like dipping your toes in the water before diving in. It allows you to monitor and learn about your email traffic without affecting deliverability, giving you time to make informed adjustments before enforcing stricter rules.

This phased approach helps organizations gradually transition to a more secure email environment without disrupting legitimate communications.

How DMARC Works

To understand how DMARC works, it is essential to see it as an added layer that integrates with SPF and DKIM to provide domain owners with greater control. DMARC involves the following key steps:

1. **Define DMARC Policy**: The domain owner publishes a DMARC policy in their DNS as a TXT record. This policy defines how receiving mail servers should handle emails that fail SPF or DKIM checks. Think of publishing a DMARC policy as putting up a sign outside your building that tells security guards what to do if an unrecognized person tries to enter — should they be let in, questioned, or outright blocked? Similarly, publishing your DMARC policy in the DNS tells email servers how to handle messages that don't pass authentication. The policy can also indicate that reports should be sent to a designated address, allowing the domain owner to monitor the effectiveness of their email authentication efforts.

2. **Email Authentication Checks**: When an email is received, the receiving mail server performs SPF and DKIM checks to authenticate the email. SPF ensures that the email is coming from an authorized sending server, and DKIM verifies that the email's content has not been tampered with. Both checks help establish that the email is legitimate and has not been altered during transmission. The combination of SPF and DKIM ensures that the sender's identity is verified and that the message content is intact.

3. **DMARC Alignment**: DMARC checks whether the authenticated domain (from SPF or DKIM) matches the domain in the "From" address. This alignment ensures that the domain in the "From" header matches what's

verified by either SPF or DKIM, or both. It's like double-checking the ID of a visitor against both a guest list and a badge. This alignment is key to preventing phishing attacks that rely on faking the sender address.

4. **Enforcement of DMARC Policy**: Based on the alignment check, the receiving server takes action according to the DMARC policy (`none`, `quarantine`, or `reject`). If the email passes the checks, it is delivered as usual. If the email fails, it will either be quarantined, rejected, or allowed, depending on the specified policy. The ability to reject or quarantine emails that fail authentication helps prevent fraudulent emails from reaching the inbox, thereby reducing the risk of phishing and other cyberattacks. This enforcement capability provides domain owners with a powerful tool to protect their brand and prevent abuse of their domain by malicious actors.

5. **Reporting**: DMARC also includes a reporting feature that allows domain owners to receive **aggregate** and **forensic** reports. Aggregate reports provide summary data about authentication results, including who is sending emails on behalf of the domain and the pass/fail status. Forensic reports provide detailed information about specific emails that failed authentication. These reports give domain owners valuable insights into email traffic and help them detect unauthorized activity. By analyzing these reports, organizations can identify patterns of abuse, unauthorized use of their domain, and opportunities to improve their email security configuration. Reports also help organizations gain visibility into their email infrastructure, identify potential misconfigurations, and take corrective actions to strengthen their overall email security posture.

> **Did you know?** DMARC reports are like security logs that tell you who's been trying to enter your building and if they succeeded or were stopped. These reports give you valuable information to identify suspicious behavior and improve your defenses.

Setting Up DMARC

Implementing DMARC involves a series of steps that require an understanding of both SPF and DKIM, as DMARC relies on these protocols for authentication:

1. **Ensure SPF and DKIM are Configured**: Before setting up DMARC, it is

crucial to have both SPF and DKIM properly configured for your domain. DMARC builds upon these protocols, so they must be in place for DMARC to function correctly. SPF helps identify authorized servers, while DKIM ensures that the email content has not been altered. Ensuring that both SPF and DKIM are properly configured is the foundation for a successful DMARC implementation.

2. **Create a DMARC Record**: To create a DMARC record, you will need to define the policy you want to enforce. Creating a DMARC record is like setting the ground rules for your security team—detailing what actions to take if someone doesn't pass the initial checks. Should they be watched, blocked, or allowed in with caution? By defining these rules clearly in the DNS, you help email servers worldwide understand your expectations. The DMARC record is published as a DNS TXT record. The key components of a DMARC record include:

   - **v**: Version of DMARC (currently always `v=DMARC1`).

   - **p**: Policy for handling emails that fail DMARC checks (`none`, `quarantine`, `reject`). Start with `p=none`.

   - **rua**: Address to which aggregate reports should be sent.

   - **ruf**: Address to which forensic reports should be sent.

   - **pct**: Percentage of emails to which the policy should be applied.

   A typical DMARC record might look like this:

```
v=DMARC1; p=none; rua=mailto:dmarc-reports@example.com;
ruf=mailto:forensic-reports@example.com; pct=100
```

   In this example:

   - **p=none**: Indicates that emails failing DMARC should be delivered.

   - **rua**: Specifies where to send aggregate reports.

   - **ruf**: Specifies where to send forensic reports.

   - **pct=100**: Indicates that the policy should be applied to 100% of emails.

By specifying a lower percentage (e.g., **pct=25**), domain owners can gradually roll out their DMARC policy to a subset of emails before applying it universally. This gradual approach helps identify any issues and allows time for troubleshooting before a full rollout. Starting with a lower percentage helps ensure that the policy does not inadvertently affect legitimate email traffic.

3. **Publish the DMARC Record**: Once the DMARC record is created, it needs to be published in your domain's DNS as a TXT record. This record will then be available to receiving servers for reference when they process emails from your domain. Proper DNS configuration is essential to ensure that the DMARC policy is accessible to receiving servers worldwide. Publishing the record correctly ensures that your DMARC policy is effective and that the domain's authentication requirements are clearly communicated.
4. **Monitor Reports and Adjust Policies**: After publishing the DMARC record, it is essential to monitor the reports that are generated. These reports provide insights into email traffic, unauthorized usage, and alignment issues. Based on the information from these reports, you can make adjustments to your SPF, DKIM, and DMARC settings to improve email authentication over time. Regularly reviewing DMARC reports allows domain owners to identify misconfigurations, unauthorized senders, and other issues that could impact the effectiveness of their email security measures. The continuous feedback provided by DMARC reports is invaluable for refining email policies, improving security, and ensuring optimal email deliverability. Consider using a DMARC report analyzer tool like **DMARCian** or **Postmark's DMARC Analyzer**. These tools present your aggregate and forensic reports in a user-friendly format, helping you quickly identify unauthorized sources and alignment issues.

Benefits of DMARC

DMARC provides a wide range of benefits that enhance email security and build trust in email communications:

- **Prevent Email Spoofing**: DMARC significantly reduces the chances of email spoofing by allowing domain owners to specify how to handle unauthenticated emails, making it harder for attackers to impersonate trusted domains. By enforcing DMARC, domain owners can ensure that only authorized servers are allowed to send emails on their behalf. This reduces the risk of phishing attacks that rely on impersonating well-known brands or organizations.

- **Protect Brand Reputation**: By preventing malicious actors from sending fraudulent emails using your domain, DMARC helps protect your brand reputation and maintain trust with your customers and partners. A compromised domain can lead to significant reputational damage, but DMARC helps to minimize this risk by verifying that only legitimate emails are being delivered. Maintaining a strong brand reputation is essential for customer trust and long-term success, and DMARC plays a critical role in safeguarding that reputation.

- **Improve Email Deliverability**: Implementing DMARC can improve email deliverability by reducing the chances of your legitimate emails being flagged as spam. Email providers are more likely to trust emails from domains with strong authentication measures, ensuring that your messages reach your intended recipients. A well-configured DMARC policy helps improve sender reputation, leading to better inbox placement for your emails. Improved deliverability translates to higher engagement rates and more effective communication with customers and stakeholders.

- **Gain Visibility into Email Traffic**: DMARC's reporting feature gives domain owners valuable insights into their email traffic. By understanding who is sending emails on behalf of their domain, organizations can detect unauthorized use and take appropriate action to stop it. This visibility is crucial for identifying misuse and proactively protecting the domain from being exploited by attackers. Reports provide transparency into how the domain is being used, which helps in making informed decisions about email policies and security measures.

- **Facilitate Continuous Improvement**: DMARC reports help identify misconfigurations, security gaps, and unauthorized use of your domain, allowing for continuous improvement. By regularly analyzing these reports, domain owners can refine their SPF, DKIM, and DMARC configurations to enhance their email security posture. This iterative process of monitoring and improvement helps ensure that email communications are secure and trustworthy, and that evolving threats are effectively mitigated.

Challenges and Best Practices for DMARC

While DMARC is a powerful tool for improving email security, it does come with some challenges that domain owners should be aware of:

- **Complex Setup**: Setting up DMARC requires a good understanding of SPF and DKIM, as well as DNS records. For organizations without in-house technical expertise, the setup process can be daunting. However, many cloud-based email providers offer tools and services to simplify DMARC implementation, making it accessible to organizations of all sizes. Leveraging these tools can help ensure a smooth setup and minimize the potential for errors.

- **Gradual Policy Enforcement**: Implementing DMARC should be a gradual process. Start with a "none" policy to collect data on your email traffic without impacting email delivery. Once you have analyzed the data and addressed any issues, gradually move to more stringent policies like "quarantine" or "reject." This phased approach helps minimize disruptions while ensuring that your domain is protected from abuse.

- **Regular Monitoring**: It is important to regularly monitor DMARC reports to identify unauthorized activity, misconfigurations, or any issues affecting email authentication. Regular monitoring helps ensure that DMARC continues to provide the intended level of protection. By staying proactive and attentive to DMARC reports, domain owners can maintain strong email security and adjust their policies to address new threats as they emerge.

- **Collaboration with Third Parties**: Many organizations use third-party vendors to send emails on their behalf. It is important to ensure that these vendors are correctly configured to pass DMARC checks, which may involve working closely with them to align SPF and DKIM records. Collaboration with third-party vendors is essential to maintaining a consistent security posture across all email communications. Ensuring that third parties follow best practices helps prevent unauthorized emails from being delivered under your domain.

- **DNS Management**: DMARC relies on DNS records for publishing policies and making them available to receiving servers. Proper DNS management is essential to avoid misconfigurations and ensure high availability. Partnering with reliable DNS providers, such as Cloudflare or GoDaddy, can help minimize the risk of DNS outages and improve the reliability of DMARC enforcement.

Conclusion

DMARC is a powerful protocol that helps domain owners protect their domains from email-based attacks such as spoofing, phishing, and impersonation. By combining SPF, DKIM, and DMARC, organizations can create a robust defense against unauthorized use of their domain, protect their brand reputation, and gain valuable insights into their email traffic.

The adoption of DMARC is crucial for anyone using custom domains who wants to ensure the integrity of their email communications and build trust with customers and partners. While the setup process may require technical expertise, the benefits—improved security, better deliverability, and enhanced visibility — make DMARC an invaluable tool in modern email security.

In the next chapter, we will discuss how to align SPF, DKIM, and DMARC effectively to create a unified email authentication strategy. This chapter will provide an in-depth guide on how these protocols work together to maximize email security. We will explore the importance of alignment, practical steps for achieving it, and troubleshooting common issues that may arise during the configuration process. Additionally, we will cover best practices for maintaining consistency across all authentication records and ensuring that your email ecosystem remains secure and efficient over time. Proper alignment of these protocols not only strengthens your domain's defenses but also improves email deliverability and enhances trust in your communications.

Action Steps

[ ] Ensure SPF and DKIM are properly implemented first.
[ ] Create a DMARC record starting with p=none to monitor activity.
[ ] Use DMARC report analyzers (e.g., Dmarcian) to review aggregate and forensic reports.
[ ] Gradually move to stricter policies (quarantine or reject) once you trust your authentication configuration.

Chapter 6: Aligning SPF, DKIM, and DMARC for Maximum Email Security

Introduction to Alignment

Think of your email security strategy as a puzzle. Each piece — SPF, DKIM, and DMARC — has its place, but the true picture emerges when all the pieces fit together perfectly. Proper alignment ensures that these protocols reinforce each other, providing a seamless layer of defense that makes your email communications more secure and trustworthy.

This chapter will cover the importance of aligning SPF, DKIM, and DMARC, as well as practical steps to achieve this alignment. We will also discuss best practices, how to troubleshoot common issues, and tips for maintaining a consistent and reliable email authentication system. By the end of this chapter, you will have a clear understanding of how to maximize your email security by leveraging the full potential of these three protocols in harmony. Proper alignment is not just about technical configuration; it also involves continuous monitoring and improvement to stay ahead of evolving threats and adapt to changes in your email infrastructure.

Importance of Alignment

The alignment of SPF, DKIM, and DMARC is crucial to creating a robust and secure email environment. Without alignment, there can be inconsistencies between different parts of your email authentication strategy, leading to vulnerabilities that attackers can exploit.

> *Did you know?* Emails that pass both SPF and DKIM checks but have misaligned domains can still be flagged as suspicious by receiving servers. Ensuring proper alignment is like confirming the credentials of a guest at a security checkpoint — everything must match to allow entry.

Proper alignment ensures that all parts of the email verification process agree on the legitimacy of the message, thereby enhancing the overall credibility of your domain.

Alignment helps achieve the following benefits:

- **Enhanced Security**: By aligning SPF, DKIM, and DMARC, you create multiple checkpoints that an email must pass before it reaches its destination. This multi-layered security makes it significantly more difficult for malicious actors to forge emails, similar to having several locked doors that must all be opened before gaining access.

- **Improved Deliverability**: Properly aligned emails are more likely to reach recipients' inboxes rather than being marked as spam or blocked. Email providers prioritize authenticated emails, which helps improve sender reputation and ensures better email deliverability. A high sender reputation increases the likelihood that your email campaigns will achieve their intended impact, leading to more successful communication efforts.

- **Consistent Email Experience**: Alignment helps maintain a consistent experience for recipients by reducing the number of false positives — legitimate emails flagged as spam. A well-aligned setup instills trust in your communications, resulting in greater confidence among recipients. This consistency also helps to reinforce brand identity, as recipients are more likely to engage with emails they trust.

Proper alignment also means that domain owners can confidently identify which emails are legitimate and which are not, helping them to protect their brand and their customers from impersonation and fraud. In addition to reducing the likelihood of false positives, alignment also ensures that messages are handled according to the specified policy, which may include rejecting or quarantining suspicious emails. This not only protects recipients but also maintains the integrity of the organization's communication channels.

Achieving Alignment: Practical Steps

Aligning SPF, DKIM, and DMARC involves ensuring that the domains used in SPF, DKIM, and the "From" header all match and point to the correct and authorized domain. Below are practical steps for achieving proper alignment:

1. **Align SPF**:

    - SPF ensures that the IP address of the sending server is authorized by the domain owner. To align SPF, the **sending server must be authorized** to send emails on behalf of the **envelope domain** (the domain in the "Return-Path" or "Mail From" field).

    - Configure SPF records in your DNS to include all IP addresses and services authorized to send emails on your behalf. Make sure the domains match or use subdomains that are clearly associated with your main domain. Proper alignment of SPF also involves reducing unnecessary entries and ensuring that only trusted servers are authorized to send emails.

    - **Consider Flattening SPF Records**: SPF records are limited to 10 DNS lookups, and exceeding this limit can cause issues with email delivery. To avoid exceeding the limit, consider flattening your SPF record by replacing "include" directives with their corresponding IP addresses. Flattening can help ensure that your SPF alignment passes while maintaining simplicity in your DNS configurations.

2. **Align DKIM**:

    - DKIM provides a digital signature to ensure that the content of an email is not altered in transit. To align DKIM, the **d= tag** in the DKIM signature must match the **domain in the "From" header** of the email.

    - Ensure that DKIM is set up correctly by generating a private-public key pair and publishing the public key in the DNS. Use consistent selectors across different services and ensure that the **d= domain** in the DKIM signature aligns with the "From" domain. Consistent DKIM selectors can simplify key management and rotation, helping maintain alignment even as email systems evolve.

    - **Key Rotation**: Regularly rotate DKIM keys to prevent attackers from exploiting any potential weaknesses. Publishing new keys and updating the DNS records helps maintain the security and reliability of DKIM signatures over time. Implementing a rotation schedule ensures that the DKIM infrastructure remains current and reduces the risk of key compromise.

3. **Publish and Test DMARC Policy**:

- A DMARC policy instructs receiving email servers on how to handle messages that fail SPF or DKIM checks. DMARC ensures that either SPF, DKIM, or both are aligned with the "From" address.

- Publish a DMARC record with a policy (`p=none`, `p=quarantine`, or `p=reject`) in your DNS. Start with a **p=none** policy to collect reports and observe the alignment results. This approach helps domain owners gather information and identify issues without immediately impacting email delivery.

- Gradually increase the enforcement level (to `quarantine` or `reject`) as you achieve proper alignment across SPF and DKIM. By moving incrementally, you can ensure that all services and systems are correctly configured before imposing strict DMARC enforcement.

- **Aggregate and Forensic Reporting**: Leverage DMARC reports to analyze email traffic and identify areas where alignment can be improved. Aggregate reports provide an overview of email traffic and alignment status, while forensic reports provide detailed insights into failed authentication attempts. These reports are valuable tools for understanding the current email landscape and making informed decisions about enforcement levels.

4. **Test and Validate Alignment**:

- Use testing tools to validate the alignment of SPF, DKIM, and DMARC. Tools like **MxToolbox, Mail-Tester**[4], and **Google Postmaster Tools**[5] can help you verify that emails are passing authentication checks and that the alignment between domains is correct. Regular testing helps

---

[4] https://www.mail-tester.com/

[5] https://www.gmail.com/postmaster/

identify potential configuration issues before they become widespread problems.

- Send test emails from different systems and services to ensure that SPF and DKIM signatures are being applied correctly and that DMARC alignment passes. Testing with multiple services can help uncover inconsistencies and ensure that all email-sending systems are properly aligned.

- **Monitor User Feedback**: In addition to technical testing, monitor feedback from recipients to determine if legitimate emails are being marked as spam or failing delivery. User feedback can provide early warnings of potential misconfigurations that need to be addressed.

Troubleshooting Common Alignment Issues

Even with careful planning, alignment issues can arise, leading to failed authentication checks. Below are some common issues and how to resolve them:

1. **SPF Failures**:

    - **Incorrect IPs in SPF Record**: Regularly review and audit your SPF records to ensure all authorized IP addresses are included. Missing entries can lead to legitimate emails failing SPF checks, much like leaving someone important off a guest list. By auditing SPF records routinely, you minimize the risk of errors.

    - **Exceeded DNS Lookup Limit**: SPF records are limited to 10 DNS lookups. If you exceed this limit, receiving servers may not process the SPF record correctly. Flatten your SPF record by replacing "include" directives with their equivalent IP addresses to reduce lookups. You can also consider using services that help optimize SPF records to stay within the lookup limit.

2. **DKIM Failures**:

    - **Mismatched Domains**: Ensure that the domain specified in the **d= tag** of the DKIM signature matches the "From" address domain. If different subdomains are used, ensure they are properly associated. Using consistent domain names and selectors helps avoid alignment issues.

- **Key Length or Expiration**: Ensure that your DKIM keys are sufficiently strong (at least 2048 bits) and not expired. Regularly rotate DKIM keys and publish updated public keys in DNS. Weak or outdated keys may fail verification, leading to failed DKIM checks and alignment issues.

- **Incorrect Key Publishing**: Verify that the public key is correctly published in your DNS as a TXT record. Mistakes in the DNS entry can lead to failed DKIM checks, even if the signing process is working correctly.

3. **DMARC Failures**:

    - **Incorrect Policy Settings**: Make sure your DMARC policy is correctly configured. Start with a **p=none** policy to monitor and adjust before moving to stricter enforcement. Incorrect settings can lead to legitimate emails being rejected or quarantined.

    - **Misaligned Domains**: Ensure that SPF aligns with the envelope domain (the domain in the "Return-Path" or "Mail From" field), while DKIM aligns with the "From" header domain. Use subdomains where appropriate, but they must be clearly related to the main domain to avoid confusion. Alignment issues can often be traced back to inconsistencies in domain naming conventions or misconfigured third-party services. Proper alignment of SPF and DKIM ensures that emails pass authentication checks, which helps prevent email spoofing and enhances the overall trustworthiness of your domain.

    - **Lack of Reporting**: If you are not receiving DMARC reports, check the **rua** and **ruf** tags in your DMARC record to ensure that they are correctly configured. Reports are essential for identifying issues and making necessary adjustments to maintain alignment.

Best Practices for Maintaining Alignment

- **Gradual Rollout**: Start with a **p=none** DMARC policy to gather data and validate alignment before increasing enforcement to `quarantine` or `reject`. This gradual approach helps avoid any disruptions in email delivery. Gradual rollout also allows you to identify and resolve alignment issues before they have a significant impact on communication.

- **Monitor Regularly**: Use DMARC reports to monitor your email authentication results continuously. Look for signs of failed alignment, unauthorized senders, or services that need to be added to SPF or DKIM configurations. Regular monitoring is essential for maintaining alignment and adapting to changes in your email environment.

- **Rotate DKIM Keys**: Regularly rotate DKIM keys to ensure ongoing security. Publish new public keys in your DNS and update mail servers accordingly to maintain alignment and security. Key rotation helps to prevent attackers from exploiting compromised keys and keeps your email system secure.

- **Coordinate with Third Parties**: Ensure that all third-party services that send emails on your behalf (e.g., marketing platforms, CRM systems) are correctly configured to align with your domain. Work with vendors to achieve proper SPF and DKIM alignment for their services. Misaligned third-party emails can negatively impact your sender reputation and lead to failed DMARC checks.

- **Maintain DNS Accuracy**: Keep DNS records updated, accurate, and accessible. Misconfigurations in DNS are a common cause of failed SPF, DKIM, or DMARC checks. Using reliable DNS management services can help minimize errors and improve overall stability. DNS accuracy is crucial for ensuring that all authentication mechanisms work as intended and that alignment is maintained.

- **Regular Audits**: Conduct regular audits of your SPF, DKIM, and DMARC configurations. Audits help ensure that all records are up-to-date and properly configured. They also help identify any new services or changes in your infrastructure that require updates to your email authentication settings.

Conclusion

Aligning SPF, DKIM, and DMARC is a fundamental step in creating a unified email authentication strategy. When these protocols are properly aligned, they provide robust protection against email-based threats, enhance the deliverability of legitimate emails, and build trust in your communications. Achieving alignment requires careful configuration, testing, and ongoing monitoring, but the payoff is significant—a secure and reliable email ecosystem that reduces the risks of phishing, spoofing, and other cyberattacks.

Proper alignment is not a one-time task; it is an ongoing process that requires regular maintenance and updates. As your organization evolves and new services are added, adjustments to SPF, DKIM, and DMARC may be necessary to maintain alignment. By following best practices, testing regularly, and using DMARC reports effectively, you can create a resilient email security strategy that keeps your organization and its stakeholders safe.

In the next chapter, we will explore real-world case studies of organizations that have successfully implemented SPF, DKIM, and DMARC. These case studies will provide insights into best practices, lessons learned, and the tangible benefits that come from having a properly aligned and enforced email security framework. Understanding these real-world examples will help you see the value of alignment in action and apply similar strategies to protect your own domain and improve the security of your email communications.

Checklist

[..].Verify that domains used in SPF, DKIM, and the "From" header align.
[..].Check DNS entries for accuracy and correct any typos or misconfigurations.
[..].Review DMARC reports to identify misaligned messages and address any issues.
[..].Test emails from various senders and services to ensure proper alignment.

Chapter 7: Real-World Case Studies of SPF, DKIM, and DMARC Implementation

Introduction to Case Studies

The real-world examples in this chapter demonstrate how major organizations — facing challenges much like your own — implemented SPF, DKIM, and DMARC to protect their brand reputation and customers. Whether you're an SMB or an enterprise, these use cases provide a detailed roadmap for securing your email channels effectively. By understanding their strategies, you can apply similar methods to safeguard your domain from malicious actors, enhance deliverability, and improve customer trust. This chapter illustrates the importance of proactive email security and shows how different approaches can be customized to fit various organizational needs.

Case Study 1: PayPal's Journey to Implement DMARC

PayPal, a leading online payment service provider, was often a target of phishing attacks, with cybercriminals attempting to trick users into providing their credentials through fake emails. The impact on their customers' trust and PayPal's brand reputation made email security a top priority, as they needed to protect their users and maintain the reliability of their services.

Challenges

Phishing emails spoofing PayPal's domain were causing significant damage, leading to customer complaints, financial losses, and reduced trust. The challenge was to implement a solution that could minimize these phishing emails while ensuring legitimate communications remained unaffected and maintaining a seamless customer experience.

Solution

PayPal decided to implement DMARC (Domain-based Message Authentication, Reporting, and Conformance) alongside SPF and DKIM to strengthen its email authentication framework. They started with a DMARC policy of "none" to collect data on their email traffic and identify authorized and unauthorized sources. This phase allowed them to observe how their email channels were being used and to make informed decisions about tightening security.

Over time, PayPal moved to stricter policies, eventually using a "reject" policy to block unauthorized emails entirely. This gradual approach allowed them to mitigate risks without disrupting legitimate communications and ensured that third-party email providers had time to align with their updated policies.

PayPal's SPF record:

```
v=spf1 include:pp._spf.paypal.com include:3ph1._spf.paypal.com
include:3ph2._spf.paypal.com include:3ph3._spf.paypal.com
include:3ph4._spf.paypal.com include:sendgrid.net
include:aspmx.pardot.com ~all
```

PayPal's DMARC record:

```
v=DMARC1 p=reject rua=mailto:d@rua.agari.com
ruf=mailto:d@ruf.agari.com
```

Results

By gradually increasing their DMARC enforcement level, PayPal reduced phishing emails using their domain significantly. Customer complaints decreased, and confidence in the security of PayPal communications improved. Additionally, PayPal observed an overall improvement in email deliverability, as email servers began to trust their domain more due to the proper implementation of authentication protocols.

Key Takeaways for Your Implementation

1. Start with a DMARC policy of 'none' to analyze email traffic while ensuring uninterrupted deliverability.

2. Work closely with third-party email providers to ensure proper alignment and compliance with your security policies.

3. Gradually move to a "quarantine" or "reject" policy as your understanding of your email traffic improves and you gain confidence in the accuracy of your authentication setup.

Case Study 2: LinkedIn's Adoption of DKIM for Email Integrity

LinkedIn, the world's largest professional network, wanted to ensure that email notifications sent to its members were secure and free from tampering. With millions of users relying on email notifications for updates, securing their communication channels was a critical focus to maintain user trust and engagement.

Challenges

LinkedIn was concerned about the possibility of cybercriminals intercepting and altering email content, compromising both user experience and security. They needed a solution that would ensure message integrity from end to end, protecting both their brand and their members from fraudulent activities.

Solution

LinkedIn implemented DomainKeys Identified Mail (DKIM) across all their outgoing email servers. DKIM provided a cryptographic signature to each email, allowing recipient servers to verify that the messages were not altered during transit. This digital signature acted as proof of authenticity, giving recipients confidence that the email content was genuine.

In addition, LinkedIn used unique DKIM selectors for different types of email traffic. This allowed them to maintain granular control and visibility over various communications, such as marketing campaigns, transactional emails, and member notifications.

LinkedIn's SPF record:

```
v=spf1 ip4:199.101.162.0/25 ip4:108.174.3.0/24
ip4:108.174.6.0/24 ip4:108.174.0.0/24 ip6:2620:109:c00d:104::/64
ip6:2620:109:c006:104::/64 ip6:2620:109:c003:104::/64
ip6:2620:119:50c0:207::/64 ip4:199.101.161.130 mx
mx:docusign.net ~all
```

LinkedIn's DMARC record:

```
v=DMARC1 p=reject rua=mailto:d@rua.agari.com,mailto:yfy3q-
9359@rua.dmarc.emailanalyst.com
ruf=mailto:d@ruf.agari.com,mailto:yfy3q-
9359@ruf.dmarc.emailanalyst.com
```

Results

The implementation of DKIM significantly reduced the risk of man-in-the-middle attacks. Members of LinkedIn could be confident that notifications from the platform were genuine and had not been altered. This helped enhance the platform's trustworthiness and improved email deliverability, as authenticated emails were more likely to bypass spam filters and reach their intended recipients.

Key Takeaways for Your Implementation

1. Ensure DKIM signing is configured for all outgoing mail servers to maintain email integrity and protect against tampering.

2. Use unique selectors for different types of email traffic to maintain better control, visibility, and effective troubleshooting.

3. Test DKIM setup with major ISPs and email platforms to ensure effective validation and seamless email delivery.

Case Study 3: Bank of America's Comprehensive Use of SPF, DKIM, and DMARC

As one of the largest financial institutions in the United States, Bank of America faced relentless phishing attacks aimed at their customers. Protecting their brand

and ensuring that customers trusted communications from the bank were crucial objectives, especially in an industry where trust and security are paramount.

Challenges

The bank faced an ongoing issue with cybercriminals attempting to spoof their domain to deceive customers into providing sensitive information. Implementing a solution that would not only authenticate legitimate emails but also block fraudulent messages was essential to maintaining customer trust and reducing the risk of data breaches.

Solution

Bank of America took a comprehensive approach by implementing SPF, DKIM, and DMARC in unison. SPF ensured that only authorized IP addresses could send emails on behalf of their domain, thereby preventing unauthorized servers from impersonating them. DKIM added a cryptographic signature to verify message integrity, and DMARC provided a final layer of policy enforcement to reject unauthorized emails and protect customers from phishing attacks.

They also leveraged DMARC reports to gain visibility into who was attempting to use their domain. By analyzing these reports, they could adjust their policies, take action against unauthorized sources, and collaborate with third-party senders to ensure compliance with their security requirements.

Bank of America's SPF record:

```
v=spf1 ip4:171.161.41.178 ip4:171.159.227.167
ip4:171.161.147.155 include:spf-0000ec08.pphosted.com
include:spf-0000ec15.pphosted.com ~all
```

Bank of America's DMARC record:

```
v=DMARC1 p=reject fo=1
rua=mailto:auth.report_ns@bankofamerica.com
ruf=mailto:bankofamerica@ruf.agari.com
```

Results

The comprehensive implementation resulted in a significant drop in phishing emails spoofing the bank's domain. Customers reported fewer suspicious emails, and Bank of America saw improved email deliverability due to the alignment of

SPF, DKIM, and DMARC. Additionally, the bank's proactive approach to monitoring DMARC reports allowed them to quickly identify and address any gaps, further enhancing their overall email security posture.

Key Takeaways for Your Implementation

1. Implement SPF, DKIM, and DMARC in unison to maximize email security and ensure comprehensive coverage.

2. Use DMARC reports to gain visibility into unauthorized use of your domain and to identify potential vulnerabilities.

3. Collaborate with third-party email senders to ensure consistent policy alignment, compliance, and seamless email authentication.

Conclusion

These real-world examples demonstrate the benefits of aligning SPF, DKIM, and DMARC. When properly implemented and enforced, these protocols can drastically reduce phishing, spoofing, and other email-based threats. They help protect brand reputation, improve email deliverability, and strengthen customer trust. Implementing these protocols also allows organizations to gain better visibility into their email ecosystem, making it easier to identify and mitigate unauthorized use of their domain.

The key takeaway is that email authentication is not just a technical exercise but a strategic move to protect your brand, your customers, and your reputation. With the right mix of technologies, proactive monitoring, and gradual policy enforcement, your organization can significantly reduce email-based threats.

In the next chapter, we will discuss emerging technologies that enhance these protocols, ensuring that your defenses remain strong against new and evolving threats. Let's continue to build a safer and more secure email communication environment together.

Action Steps

[ ] Identify which case study is most similar to your organization's situation.
[ ] Note the key tactics (e.g., gradual DMARC enforcement, key rotation) and consider applying them.

[ ] Reach out to third-party senders or vendors to improve coordination in implementing these protocols.

Chapter 8: The Future of Email Security

Introduction

In previous chapters, we explored the critical role that email authentication protocols like SPF, DKIM, and DMARC play in securing email communications. While these protocols form the foundation of email security, the evolving landscape demands even more advanced strategies to tackle increasingly sophisticated threats. In this chapter, we will explore some of the key trends and technologies shaping the future of email security.

The future of email security is all about adaptation, innovation, and leveraging smarter technology to outpace cyber threats. From AI-driven threat detection to quantum-proof cryptography, the landscape is evolving, and understanding these changes is crucial to staying secure. This chapter will not only highlight the newest and most promising advancements in email security but also help you understand the practical implications for your organization, including the potential benefits and challenges.

Key Trends and Technologies in Email Security

1. **Artificial Intelligence (AI) and Machine Learning (ML)**

    - AI and ML are becoming essential tools in the fight against email threats. These technologies can analyze vast amounts of email data, learning to recognize patterns that indicate phishing, spoofing, or malware. Instead of relying solely on static rules, AI can adapt to new attack tactics in real-time. For instance, AI can identify and block phishing campaigns that use slight variations of domain names (e.g., substituting similar-looking characters) which traditional filters might miss. This dynamic approach allows security systems to evolve in tandem with cyber threats.

- **Behavioral Analysis**: AI can track normal email usage patterns for individual users and flag anomalies. For instance, if an employee typically communicates with a known set of contacts, an email from an unfamiliar address requesting sensitive information would be flagged as suspicious. This helps catch sophisticated attacks that might evade traditional rule-based systems.

- **Automation**: AI also enhances automation in responding to email threats. By automating tasks like email filtering and quarantining, organizations can quickly mitigate risks without human intervention, freeing up cybersecurity personnel for more complex challenges. AI-powered automation can significantly reduce response times, which is crucial for preventing the spread of malware and minimizing damage from targeted attacks.

- **AI for Threat Hunting**: Advanced AI systems are being used to hunt for threats before they become a problem. These systems can proactively identify emerging trends and anomalies across the organization's email communications, enabling a more proactive stance against threats.

2. **Cloud-Based Email Security Solutions**

- As organizations increasingly adopt cloud-based email services like Microsoft 365 and Google Workspace, cloud-based security solutions have gained prominence. These solutions are scalable, regularly updated, and can protect against sophisticated email attacks without requiring on-premises infrastructure. Unlike traditional on-premises email security solutions, cloud-based options are designed for rapid adaptability, allowing businesses to quickly adjust their defenses to meet evolving security needs without the constraints of physical hardware. Additionally, cloud-based solutions can often be more cost-effective, reducing the need for investments in physical hardware and ongoing maintenance.

- **Centralized Management**: Cloud-based email security tools provide a centralized platform for managing email security across multiple domains and services. This helps simplify administration, making it easier for IT teams to maintain strong security policies. Centralized management also allows for consistent security practices and streamlined policy enforcement, reducing the risk of misconfigurations.

- **Real-Time Threat Intelligence**: Many cloud-based platforms benefit from integrated real-time threat intelligence, allowing them to instantly react to emerging threats seen across their networks globally. This capability is particularly important for organizations facing advanced persistent threats (APTs), as global threat intelligence enables rapid identification and mitigation of new attack vectors.

- **Scalability and Flexibility**: Cloud solutions offer flexibility and can easily scale to accommodate organizational growth. As a company expands or contracts, its email security infrastructure can be adjusted accordingly without the need for significant capital expenditure or downtime.

3. Zero Trust Approach to Email

    - The concept of **Zero Trust** is becoming increasingly significant in email security. Zero Trust means treating every email as potentially malicious until proven otherwise. This approach operates on the principle of 'never trust, always verify,' ensuring that each email communication passes strict checks before being allowed access. Zero Trust emphasizes multi-factor authentication (MFA), strict access controls, and continuous monitoring to ensure email security.

    - **Verification Layers**: For email, a Zero Trust approach involves verifying the identity of both the sender and recipient before any sensitive information is exchanged. This may include **digital certificates, encryption**, and **multi-step verification processes** to establish trust. The layered verification approach ensures that even if one security layer fails, other mechanisms remain in place to prevent unauthorized access.

    - **Segmentation**: Zero Trust also implies network segmentation —

ensuring that even if an email threat breaches one part of the network, it cannot easily spread to others. This limits the impact of successful attacks. By segmenting critical resources and maintaining strict access controls, organizations can minimize the damage caused by compromised credentials or phishing attacks.

- **Continuous Validation**: Zero Trust involves continuously validating all transactions and communication. Instead of a one-time verification, systems and communications are constantly monitored to ensure compliance with security policies. This approach reduces the window of opportunity for attackers who gain initial access.

4. **Emerging Protocols and Standards**

- To keep pace with cyber threats, new standards and protocols are being developed to enhance email security.

- **BIMI (Brand Indicators for Message Identification)**: BIMI is an emerging standard that allows verified brands to display their logos directly in recipients' inboxes. This helps users identify legitimate emails and enhances trust. BIMI works alongside DMARC to verify that the email actually comes from the brand it claims to represent. BIMI provides a visual indicator that the email is legitimate, which can enhance user engagement and reduce the likelihood of phishing.

- **MTA-STS (Mail Transfer Agent Strict Transport Security)**: MTA-STS is a protocol designed to improve the security of SMTP (the protocol for email transmission). It helps ensure that emails are only sent over encrypted channels, reducing the risk of interception and man-in-the-middle attacks. As email remains a major vector for data breaches, MTA-STS provides an additional layer of protection by ensuring encryption during transit

- **TLS-RPT (TLS Reporting)**: TLS-RPT is a reporting mechanism that allows email senders to receive reports about issues encountered when establishing encrypted email connections using MTA-STS. This allows organizations to gain insights into any problems with email encryption, helping them identify potential weaknesses and improve their email security posture

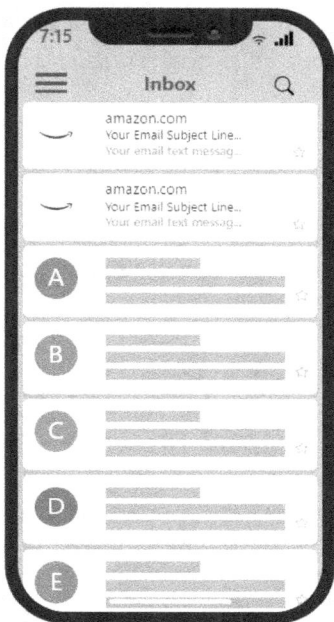

Figure 6: Amazon uses BIMI to display logo in recipients' inboxes

5. **Post-Quantum Cryptography**

- As quantum computing technology advances, it is expected to eventually break many of the encryption methods that are currently used for email security. Post-quantum cryptography is being developed to counteract this threat by creating encryption algorithms that even quantum computers cannot easily break.

- **Future-Proofing Email Encryption**: Although quantum computing is still in its infancy, some organizations are already taking steps to future-proof their email systems. By adopting post-quantum encryption protocols, they aim to stay ahead of potential quantum-powered threats. Organizations that prepare now will be better positioned to maintain security as quantum computing becomes more accessible. This preparation is especially crucial for industries like finance and healthcare, where data security is paramount, and the consequences of encryption failures can be particularly damaging.

- **Hybrid Solutions**: To bridge the gap between current encryption and future quantum-resistant standards, hybrid cryptographic solutions are being developed. These solutions combine traditional encryption with quantum-safe algorithms, providing added layers of security until post-quantum standards become widely adopted.

- **Government and Industry Initiatives**: Governments and large corporations are investing in research on post-quantum cryptography, highlighting the importance of preparing for a quantum future. These initiatives will help shape the standards and best practices that organizations can adopt to secure their communications.

6. User Awareness and Training

- While technology plays a crucial role, user awareness and training remain essential components of email security. Many cyberattacks exploit human behavior—such as clicking on a malicious link or downloading an attachment from an unknown sender.

- **Gamified Training Programs**: To keep employees engaged, organizations are increasingly adopting gamified training programs that turn learning about email security into a rewarding experience. Training modules can include quizzes, interactive scenarios, and rewards for successful completion. This approach helps make training more memorable and effective, encouraging employees to adopt secure behaviors.

- **Phishing Simulations**: Simulated phishing campaigns continue to be one of the most effective ways to assess and improve user awareness. By regularly exposing employees to simulated attacks, organizations can identify gaps in knowledge and take corrective action before a real attack occurs. These simulations help build a culture of security within the organization, where employees are vigilant and proactive.

- **Ongoing Education**: Email threats evolve, and so must user education. Regular, ongoing education sessions that keep employees informed about the latest email scams and tactics used by cybercriminals are crucial. A well-informed workforce is less likely to fall victim to sophisticated attacks.

7. **Enhanced Email Authentication**

    - Email authentication protocols like SPF, DKIM, and DMARC will continue to play a vital role in securing email. However, improvements and enhancements to these protocols are on the horizon.

    - **Greater Adoption of DMARC Enforcement**: Despite the effectiveness of DMARC, many organizations still do use "none" policies, which do not take action against unauthorized emails. In the future, we expect to see increased adoption of stricter DMARC policies, such as "quarantine" or "reject," to better protect against phishing and spoofing. Stricter enforcement can help prevent unauthorized use of domains, significantly reducing the risk of brand impersonation.

    - **Automated Configuration and Monitoring**: New tools are being developed to simplify the deployment and monitoring of email authentication protocols. Automated solutions can help organizations configure SPF, DKIM, and DMARC correctly, minimizing human error and ensuring continuous protection. These tools can also provide alerts when there are misconfigurations or unauthorized changes, helping organizations stay ahead of threats.

    - **Improved Reporting and Insights**: Enhanced reporting capabilities for email authentication will allow organizations to gain deeper insights into who is attempting to misuse their domain. Improved DMARC reports can provide more detailed information about failed authentication attempts, helping organizations take targeted action to mitigate threats.

What Organizations Can Do Today to Prepare for the Future

The future of email security may involve advanced technologies, but organizations can take meaningful steps today to prepare for these changes and build a more resilient defense against evolving threats.

- **Adopt AI-Powered Email Security**: Implement solutions that use artificial intelligence and machine learning to detect and respond to threats in real-time. These solutions are adaptive and provide an extra layer of protection against sophisticated phishing and malware attacks. AI-powered security systems can also learn from past incidents, continually improving their ability to identify and block emerging threats.

- **Embrace Cloud Security Solutions**: Evaluate your organization's current on-premises infrastructure to identify areas where cloud-based email security can improve efficiency and reduce costs. By conducting a cost-benefit analysis, you can make an informed decision on moving to the cloud. Cloud security solutions provide easier management and help ensure your organization benefits from the latest threat intelligence. Additionally, cloud solutions reduce the burden on IT teams by handling updates and patching, allowing them to focus on other security initiatives.

- **Implement a Zero Trust Model**: Apply a Zero Trust approach to email by verifying every sender and every message. This involves using multiple layers of verification, strong access controls, and segmenting your network to limit exposure in the event of an attack. Zero Trust reduces the attack surface and ensures that even if one part of the network is compromised, the rest remains secure.

- **Stay Up-to-Date with Emerging Protocols**: Keep an eye on emerging protocols like BIMI and MTA-STS. Implementing these standards will help protect against evolving threats while improving user trust and experience. Staying ahead of protocol adoption also ensures that your organization remains compliant with industry best practices and can take advantage of the latest advancements in email security.

- **Invest in Post-Quantum Research**: While quantum threats may seem distant, it's essential to start thinking about the future of encryption. Monitor the development of post-quantum cryptography and begin assessing how your organization can integrate these new technologies into its infrastructure. Proactively planning for quantum-resistant encryption will help ensure that your email security remains strong in the face of future challenges.

- **Educate Your Employees**: Continue to make user awareness and training a core component of your security strategy. Employees are the first line of defense, and equipping them with the knowledge they need to spot threats will help prevent successful attacks. Make training programs engaging and update them regularly to reflect the latest threats and tactics used by attackers.

- **Strengthen Email Authentication**: Move towards stricter DMARC policies to reduce your risk of email-based attacks. By enforcing "quarantine" or "reject" policies, you can help ensure that only authenticated emails reach your recipients' inboxes. Additionally, automate the monitoring of your email authentication protocols to ensure they are consistently configured correctly and providing the desired level of protection.

Conclusion

The future of email security is dynamic, shaped by emerging technologies and evolving threats. Embracing artificial intelligence, cloud solutions, Zero Trust, and emerging protocols can significantly bolster defenses against sophisticated attacks. However, user education remains an irreplaceable cornerstone of effective email security.

To stay ahead of cybercriminals, organizations must proactively adopt new technologies, remain informed about industry standards, and continually educate their users. By implementing these strategies now, businesses can lay a solid foundation for a resilient email security posture that adapts to future threats.

In the next chapter, we will explore practical strategies for integrating these advancements into your existing email infrastructure, ensuring that your defenses are robust and adaptable in the face of ongoing change

Action Steps

[ ] Monitor emerging technologies (AI, BIMI, MTA-STS) and consider pilot testing those most relevant to you.
[ ] Subscribe to threat intelligence newsletters or follow industry groups to stay updated.
[ ] Begin discussing post-quantum cryptography or Zero Trust approaches with your security team..

Chapter 9: Integrating Email Security Advancements into Your Infrastructure

Introduction

As we've discussed in earlier chapters, email is one of the most essential yet vulnerable communication tools for any organization. Integrating advanced security measures into your infrastructure is key to protecting this critical channel. In this chapter, we'll take a practical approach to help you use emerging technologies effectively while building upon the core protocols — SPF, DKIM, and DMARC — that we've already explored.

Our aim is not to overwhelm you with technical jargon but to inspire proactive steps toward safeguarding your organization's most vital communication channel. Email security shouldn't be about creating barriers that slow you down; it should be about building confidence and agility to keep your organization one step ahead of attackers.

Understanding Your Current Position

Before diving into new security measures, you need a clear understanding of your current email security landscape. Take stock of where you stand. Are protections like SPF, DKIM, and DMARC properly set up? Are employees aware of potential threats, or do they struggle to spot phishing attempts? Conducting a thorough audit helps you identify weak spots in your defenses and prioritize what needs improvement.

Think of this process like assessing the foundation of your house before upgrading to a more sophisticated security system. By identifying weaknesses in your current email security setup, you can systematically address them and build a stronger foundation for future improvements.

Leveraging AI for Smarter Defense

Artificial intelligence is not just a buzzword — it's a game changer for email security. AI-powered tools can analyze thousands of messages in real time, learning to identify what looks suspicious and adapting to new tactics used by attackers. Instead of being reactive, you can get ahead of threats before they become a problem.

Imagine having a security system that knows the habits of your entire organization. When something deviates from the norm, it instantly raises a red flag. AI can filter out spam, detect anomalies, and even quarantine suspicious emails, freeing up your IT team to focus on bigger-picture threats instead of firefighting every day.

For example, AI tools like Microsoft Defender for Office 365 or Google's AI-powered threat protection can analyze thousands of messages in real time, flagging anomalies based on evolving threat patterns. This proactive approach means AI is not just filtering spam but also adapting to the latest attack techniques before they become an issue

Start with a pilot program: implement an AI-based solution with one department and see how well it integrates. Automation is your ally here — let AI handle repetitive tasks like spam filtering, while your team focuses on analyzing sophisticated threats. Over time, AI will learn and improve, becoming an increasingly effective tool in your security arsenal.

Adopting Cloud-Based Email Security Solutions

Moving to the cloud might feel like a big leap, but it brings immense benefits for email security. A cloud-based solution is scalable, easy to manage, and continuously updated. Plus, it allows your team to focus less on maintaining infrastructure and more on proactive defense.

Cloud-based email security solutions are especially beneficial for SMBs that may lack the resources for extensive on-premises infrastructure. These solutions provide enterprise-grade security without the overhead, making sophisticated defenses accessible to smaller organizations.

Cloud solutions not only save time but also provide resilience. If your on-premises systems are compromised or go down, a cloud-based email security solution ensures continuity. In an age where remote work is the norm, having a cloud-first approach is an effective way to keep your communication channels secure, regardless of where your team is located.

Embrace the Zero Trust Model

Embracing a Zero Trust model means verifying the authenticity of every email communication, treating every message with skepticism until proven safe. Multi-Factor Authentication (MFA) and ongoing access verification ensure that even if a breach occurs, damage is minimized.

Multi-Factor Authentication (MFA) is a crucial part of this puzzle — especially for privileged email accounts. Adding layers of verification ensures that even if a password is compromised, unauthorized access is still prevented. Combine MFA with network segmentation so that if an attacker breaches one part of your system, they can't easily access the rest. Zero Trust isn't about being paranoid; it's about safeguarding what matters most by ensuring that trust is earned, not assumed.

The Zero Trust model also means continuously verifying access. Just because someone gets in once doesn't mean they have carte blanche forever. Verification should be ongoing, making sure that access rights are appropriate and updated as roles change. This mindset helps you minimize potential risks and contain threats before they spread.

Strengthening Email Authentication

If email security is a fortress, then email authentication is its gatekeeper. Without strong authentication, anyone can pretend to be someone they're not. Strengthening your defenses involves regularly auditing SPF, DKIM, and DMARC configurations for alignment. This means ensuring that your policies are up-to-date, your records are correctly configured, and unauthorized attempts are swiftly dealt with. Tools like DMARC Analyzer can help automate this monitoring and make adjustments seamless, ensuring that you stay ahead of any attempts at domain spoofing.

Proper email authentication also protects your brand's reputation. Imagine a scenario where someone impersonates your company to send phishing emails to your clients. Without strong authentication, this could lead to loss of trust, legal issues, and a damaged reputation. By implementing strict DMARC, SPF, and DKIM policies, you help ensure your brand's identity is protected.

Exploring Emerging Protocols

The email landscape is constantly changing, and new protocols are emerging to help you stay ahead of the game. Implementing BIMI (Brand Indicators for Message Identification) adds a visual cue — your brand's logo — to help users instantly recognize genuine emails from you. This not only strengthens trust but also makes your emails stand out in a crowded inbox, enhancing brand visibility.

MTA-STS and TLS-RPT are other valuable protocols to consider. They help ensure your emails are sent securely, reducing the risk of interception, and provide insights if something goes wrong. These emerging standards offer extra layers of protection without complicating the user experience, making your email communications safer and more reliable.

Adopting these protocols shows a commitment to security and transparency. Customers and partners appreciate knowing that your organization is using the latest methods to protect sensitive information. It's about staying ahead of attackers while also showing your audience that their safety is a top priority.

AI-Powered Threat Hunting and Automated Response

Imagine if, instead of waiting for an alert, your security system actively hunted threats before they could do damage. That's the power of AI-driven threat hunting. By integrating AI solutions with your existing email tools, you can identify threats early—often before any harm is done.

AI-driven threat hunting shifts the paradigm from reactive defense to proactive identification. Instead of waiting for alerts, AI hunts down potential threats before they escalate. For example, tools like CrowdStrike Falcon and Cisco Secure Email detect and mitigate anomalies, ensuring threats are quarantined and investigated before any harm is done.

Automated responses add another layer of defense. When a suspicious email is detected, it can be quarantined instantly. Alerts are sent out, allowing your security team to investigate without delay. Over time, AI tools should adapt and learn from each incident, refining their responses to new types of threats. This isn't just reactive defense—it's proactive, dynamic, and constantly evolving.

Fostering a Security-Aware Culture

No matter how sophisticated your security technology is, people are your first line of defense. Employees need to be aware of the risks, trained to spot phishing attempts, and encouraged to report anything suspicious. But let's be real — security training can be dry and uninspiring. So, make it engaging.

Gamify your training. Offer rewards to those who complete courses or successfully identify phishing simulations. Create a culture where security is part of everyday thinking, not just a box-ticking exercise. And remember, it starts from the top — when leadership visibly supports security initiatives, it sends a powerful message across the organization.

A security-aware culture also relies on open communication. Employees should feel comfortable reporting suspicious activities without fear of repercussions. Mistakes happen, and when employees are encouraged to report them promptly, it helps the organization respond more effectively.

Leaders must take an active role in fostering a security-first culture. When executives participate in training exercises and acknowledge employees who spot potential threats, it creates a ripple effect across the organization. Celebrating these 'small wins' reinforces that security is everyone's responsibility, not just the IT team's.

Collaborate with Vendors and Partners

You're not alone in this. Your email security is only as strong as the weakest link, and that often involves third-party vendors. Make sure your partners are following best practices. Develop a checklist of security practices for your vendors and conduct regular assessments. Ask them to provide evidence of their SPF, DKIM, and DMARC policies, and verify their compliance periodically. If a vendor isn't meeting your standards, provide guidance on necessary improvements or consider alternatives. The goal is a unified front, where all partners are as committed to email security as your organization is.

Establish clear expectations from the start and regularly assess vendor security practices. Think of your vendors as an extension of your team — everyone has to play by the same rules to keep the organization safe. If a vendor isn't meeting your security standards, work with them to improve, or find a partner who takes security as seriously as you do.

The reality is, third-party breaches can have a direct impact on your organization's reputation. By actively engaging with vendors and ensuring they comply with your security standards, you minimize the risk of an external vulnerability becoming your problem. Collaboration and transparency are key — both within your organization and with external partners.

Planning for Future Scalability and Threats

Email security isn't a "set it and forget it" solution. The threat landscape is always changing, and your defenses need to keep up. Choose solutions that are flexible enough to grow with your organization — cloud-based platforms are a great choice because they can adapt easily as you expand.

Stay informed about new threats and industry trends. Subscribe to threat intelligence services, attend webinars, and participate in industry discussions. This knowledge keeps you prepared for what's coming next and ensures that you're not caught off guard by new types of attacks. Make continuous learning a part of your security strategy.

Also, always have a well-tested incident response plan. Knowing exactly what to do in the event of an attack can mean the difference between a minor hiccup and a major crisis. Practice your response plan regularly — tabletop exercises can help ensure everyone knows their role and is ready to act if the worst happens. Planning for future threats isn't just about technology; it's about readiness, adaptability, and the ability to respond effectively.

Conclusion

Integrating advanced email security measures into your infrastructure is crucial to defending against evolving threats. This isn't about making email security more complicated — it's about making it effective and adaptable. By embracing AI, adopting Zero Trust, strengthening authentication, and fostering a security-aware culture, you empower your organization to communicate securely and confidently. The strategies outlined in this chapter lay a solid foundation for robust email security, and the effort is well worth the peace of mind it brings.

In the next chapter, we will focus on how to continuously improve your email security posture. We'll explore strategies for staying proactive, regularly assessing effectiveness, and making incremental changes that ensure you're always one step ahead in a constantly shifting cybersecurity landscape.

Checklist

[ ] Conduct a thorough audit of your current email security posture.
[ ] Pilot an AI-driven email security tool or a cloud-based solution.
[ ] Review vendor relationships and request proof of their email authentication practices.
[ ] Update training materials to incorporate new protocols or policies (e.g., BIMI, Zero Trust).

Chapter 10: Continuous Improvement and Future-Proofing Email Security

Introduction

The landscape of email security is constantly shifting, with new threats emerging and existing tactics evolving. Simply setting up email defenses isn't enough — you need a strategy for continuously improving those defenses and adapting to future challenges. This final chapter is all about keeping your organization agile and resilient, ready to meet whatever comes next. We'll explore practical ways to maintain and future-proof your email security, ensuring that your organization is always a step ahead of potential attackers.

The key here is ongoing effort. While setting up robust email defenses is a fantastic first step, staying protected means maintaining a posture of vigilance and continuous learning. Let's dive into what that looks like in practice.

Regular Assessments and Audits

Email security is not a one-time project but an ongoing journey. Regularly assessing your defenses is essential to ensure they continue to meet your organization's needs and keep up with emerging threats. Schedule routine security audits—every quarter is a good starting point—to review your protocols, analyze threat trends, and identify areas for improvement.

During these audits, revisit the configurations of SPF, DKIM, and DMARC. Are they still optimized, or have new gaps emerged? Check whether your authentication settings are up to date, and adjust them based on recent attack patterns. If you've implemented new tools, how are they performing? An audit is also an opportunity to gather feedback from employees—are they still aware of how to handle suspicious emails, or do they need a refresher? This cycle of assessment and adjustment helps your defenses stay sharp.

Adapting to Emerging Threats

Cybercriminals are always coming up with new tricks, which means your email security strategy should always be evolving. Stay informed about new types of attacks, vulnerabilities, and best practices by subscribing to cybersecurity newsletters, participating in webinars, and joining industry forums. The more informed you are, the better equipped you'll be to adapt your defenses.

Consider dedicating time each month to reviewing threat intelligence reports. These insights can provide early warnings about emerging threats that could target your industry. Armed with this knowledge, you can take proactive steps to reinforce your email security infrastructure before attackers have a chance to exploit any weaknesses.

Employee Training and Awareness

Technology alone isn't enough to safeguard your email systems. Your employees are a crucial part of your defense, and keeping them engaged and informed should be a priority. Phishing attacks, for example, often exploit human error—someone clicking on a link or downloading an attachment without realizing it's dangerous. The better trained your staff is, the less likely they are to fall for these tactics.

Instead of the traditional, dull security training sessions, keep things engaging. Incorporate regular phishing simulations and make it fun by rewarding those who correctly identify and report threats. Host interactive workshops where employees can learn to recognize the signs of a phishing email, and encourage open communication when mistakes happen. The goal is to foster a culture where security is everyone's responsibility and learning is continuous.

Embrace Automation for Efficiency

As your email environment evolves, so will the volume of threats. Manual processes just won't cut it anymore. Embrace automation to make your security efforts more efficient and effective. Automated threat detection and response tools can do the heavy lifting—identifying suspicious activities, quarantining threats, and sending alerts—so your team can focus on more strategic initiatives.

Automation also reduces the likelihood of human error, which is often a factor in security incidents. By integrating automated tools with AI-powered threat analysis, you can proactively identify potential risks and act on them in real-time. This not only saves time but also significantly reduces the window of opportunity for attackers.

Reviewing and Enhancing Policies

Your email security policies should be living documents, not static ones that get filed away and forgotten. As your organization grows, shifts focus, or adopts new technologies, those changes need to be reflected in your security policies. Make it a habit to revisit these policies at least annually, if not more frequently.

For example, if you've recently implemented new cloud-based tools, your policies should outline how to securely interact with those tools. Or, if more employees are working remotely, your policies should be updated to cover best practices for accessing email outside the office network. The goal is to make sure that policies are clear, relevant, and easy to follow, so that they guide behavior effectively.

Building a Resilient Incident Response Plan

No matter how robust your defenses, incidents can still happen. The key to minimizing damage is having a solid incident response plan. This plan should include clear steps for what to do if an email-based attack is successful, who to contact, and how to communicate with affected parties.

Conduct regular drills—tabletop exercises—to test your incident response plan and identify any gaps. Make sure everyone knows their role, and refine the plan based on what you learn from these exercises. A strong response plan can mean the difference between a minor breach and a major crisis, and it will also boost your team's confidence in handling potential issues.

Partnering with Security Experts

You don't have to do it all alone. Partnering with external security experts can give you access to specialized knowledge and resources that might not be available in-house. Managed security service providers (MSSPs), for example, can offer monitoring, threat intelligence, and rapid response capabilities, helping you stay ahead of threats.

Collaboration with industry peers is also invaluable. Sharing information about threats and successful defense strategies can help build a stronger collective defense against cyberattacks. Consider joining information-sharing groups specific to your industry—these communities are often a goldmine of practical advice and insights.

Future-Proofing with Emerging Technologies

The future of email security is already taking shape with technologies like post-quantum cryptography, more sophisticated AI-driven defenses, and even blockchain-based verification. While some of these technologies might not be immediately necessary, keeping an eye on their development and planning for their potential integration is a great way to future-proof your defenses.

Consider investing in scalable solutions that are flexible enough to integrate future advancements. For instance, AI-driven tools that learn and adapt can continue to evolve as threats change, keeping your defenses relevant. Post-quantum cryptography might seem far off, but planning for encryption that withstands quantum computing is forward-thinking that will pay off in the long run.

Encouraging a Culture of Continuous Improvement

The most effective email security strategies are those that evolve over time. Foster a culture of continuous improvement by integrating security into daily discussions. Celebrate small wins—like employees spotting and reporting phishing attempts—and use each incident as a learning opportunity to improve.

Encourage your IT and security teams to stay curious. Provide opportunities for professional development, whether through training, attending conferences, or obtaining certifications. The more informed and skilled your team is, the stronger your email security posture will be.

Conclusion

Continuous improvement is the cornerstone of effective email security. With threats evolving constantly, maintaining a strong security posture requires regular assessments, adaptive policies, effective use of automation, and ongoing education. Your journey doesn't end when your security measures are implemented—that's just the beginning. It's about maintaining vigilance, encouraging curiosity, and fostering a culture where security is seen as a shared responsibility.

By embracing regular audits, adapting to new threats, automating where possible, and empowering your employees, you are setting the stage for a resilient and future-proof email security infrastructure. The strategies we've covered throughout this book will help your organization not just defend against today's threats, but also stay prepared for whatever comes next.

The journey of mastering email security is ongoing, but with the right mindset, tools, and commitment to continuous improvement, you'll always be ready to face the future confidently—one secure email at a time.

Action Steps

[ ] Schedule regular quarterly or semi-annual security audits and assessments.
[ ] Implement phishing simulations and track results over time.
[ ] Continuously refine policies and incident response plans based on lessons learned.
[ ] Encourage ongoing professional development for your security team and maintain a culture of continuous improvement.

Glossary of Terms

A

A Record (DNS A Record):
A type of DNS record that maps a domain name to an IPv4 address. Used by mail servers to determine where to direct email traffic.

Aggregate Reports (DMARC):
Summary reports sent by receiving mail servers to domain owners, detailing how emails from their domain were authenticated and handled over a given period. These reports help identify patterns of unauthorized email usage.

AI (Artificial Intelligence):
Computer systems that can perform tasks requiring human intelligence, such as pattern recognition and decision-making. In email security, AI can detect threats by learning from large volumes of data and adapting to new attack methods.

Alignment (DMARC Alignment):
The requirement that the domain used in an email's "From" header matches (or aligns with) the domains used in SPF and/or DKIM checks. Proper alignment ensures authenticity and prevents spoofing.

Authentication:
The process of verifying that an email is from the stated sender and has not been tampered with. Protocols like SPF, DKIM, and DMARC are used to authenticate email messages.

B

Baiting (Social Engineering):
A technique where attackers entice victims with a tempting offer (such as a USB drive labeled "Confidential Data") to trick them into unwittingly initiating a cyberattack.

BEC (Business Email Compromise):
A type of targeted phishing attack where criminals impersonate executives or trusted business partners to trick employees into sending money or sensitive information.

BIMI (Brand Indicators for Message Identification):
An emerging standard that allows verified brands to display their logos in recipients' inboxes. This visual indicator helps users distinguish legitimate messages from spoofed ones.

bh (DKIM Body Hash):
A field within the DKIM-Signature header that contains a hash value of the email's body. Even minor alterations to the message content will change the hash, invalidating the signature.

C

Certificate (Digital Certificate):
A digital document used to prove the identity of a server or user in encryption and authentication protocols, often issued by a trusted Certificate Authority (CA).

Cloud-Based Email Security:
Email security solutions hosted in the cloud, offering scalability, easy maintenance, and real-time threat intelligence without on-premises infrastructure.

Cryptographic Keys (Public and Private Keys):
A pair of keys used in cryptography. The private key is kept secret by the domain owner and used to sign emails (as in DKIM), while the public key is published in DNS records so that recipients can verify the signature.

D

Data Breach:
An incident where unauthorized individuals access confidential or sensitive information, often resulting in financial, reputational, or regulatory consequences.

Deepfake:
A manipulated audio or video that uses AI to mimic real individuals. In email security, a "deepfake voicemail" might trick users into trusting fraudulent requests.

DNC Breach (Democratic National Committee Breach):
A notable phishing-related breach in 2016 where attackers used spear-phishing to gain access to sensitive political emails, illustrating the impact of targeted email attacks.

DNS (Domain Name System):
The internet's phonebook, translating human-readable domain names (like example.com) into IP addresses. DNS is essential for publishing SPF, DKIM, and DMARC records.

DNS Lookup Limit (SPF):
SPF checks are limited to 10 DNS lookups to prevent excessive resource use. Exceeding this limit can cause emails to fail SPF validation.

DNS TXT Record:
A type of DNS record used to store text-based information. SPF, DKIM, and DMARC records are commonly published as TXT records.

DKIM (DomainKeys Identified Mail):
An email authentication protocol that uses digital signatures to verify that an email's content has not been altered during transit and that it comes from the claimed domain.

DKIM Selector:
A label that identifies a specific DKIM key record in DNS. Using selectors allows domain owners to use multiple keys and rotate them without disrupting the entire email system.

DMARC (Domain-based Message Authentication, Reporting & Conformance):
A protocol built on SPF and DKIM that allows domain owners to define policies

on how to handle emails that fail authentication and receive detailed reports about email activity.

E

Encryption:
The process of converting information into an unreadable format to prevent unauthorized access. While DKIM ensures authenticity, separate encryption methods (like TLS) ensure privacy.

F

Fo=1 (DMARC):
A DMARC tag that instructs the receiving server to generate a forensic (detailed) report when an email fails both SPF and DKIM checks.

Forensic Reports (DMARC):
Highly detailed reports sent to domain owners regarding specific messages that failed DMARC authentication. These reports can help diagnose problems or unauthorized use.

Forwarding (Email Forwarding):
The practice of redirecting an incoming email to another address. SPF can fail if the forwarder's IP is not authorized. DKIM can mitigate this issue by verifying message integrity.

H

Hashing:
A one-way cryptographic function that converts data into a fixed-length string (hash). Used in DKIM to ensure message integrity.

I

Incident Response Plan:

A predefined strategy for how an organization handles and recovers from a cybersecurity incident, such as an email-based attack or breach.

Include Mechanism (SPF):
An SPF directive that allows a domain to incorporate another domain's SPF record, commonly used when employing third-party email services.

IP Address:
A numerical label assigned to devices on a network. SPF uses IP addresses to determine if an email server is authorized to send mail for a specific domain.

M

Machine Learning (ML):
A subset of AI that involves "training" algorithms on large datasets so they can identify patterns and make decisions without explicit programming. Used in email security to recognize and respond to evolving threats.

Malware:
Malicious software (viruses, worms, ransomware) often delivered via email attachments or links, designed to disrupt systems, steal data, or demand ransoms.

MFA (Multi-Factor Authentication):
A security approach requiring multiple forms of verification (e.g., password + phone code) to confirm a user's identity, reducing the impact of stolen credentials.

MTA (Mail Transfer Agent):
A software application that routes and delivers email messages between mail servers.

MTA-STS (Mail Transfer Agent Strict Transport Security):
A protocol that enforces encrypted transmission of emails between mail servers, ensuring that emails cannot be easily intercepted or tampered with in transit.

N

None Policy (DMARC):
A DMARC policy option (p=none) that does not actively quarantine or reject

failing messages. Instead, it collects reports for monitoring email traffic and domain usage.

P

Phishing:
A social engineering tactic where attackers send fraudulent emails posing as reputable entities to trick victims into revealing sensitive information or performing harmful actions.

Post-Quantum Cryptography:
Encryption methods designed to remain secure against quantum computing capabilities, ensuring long-term protection of encrypted communications.

Private Key:
In DKIM and other cryptographic systems, the private key is kept secret by the domain owner and used to create digital signatures that can be verified by the corresponding public key.

Public Key:
A cryptographic key that is publicly available (usually via DNS) to verify signatures made by the corresponding private key. Used in DKIM to validate the authenticity of a signed email.

Q

Quarantine (DMARC Policy):
A DMARC policy option (p=quarantine) that directs emails failing authentication checks into the recipient's spam or junk folder rather than outright rejecting them.

R

Reject (DMARC Policy):
A DMARC policy option (p=reject) that drop/block emails failing authentication checks.

Replay Attack:
A type of attack where a valid email is intercepted and resent multiple times. While DKIM can confirm authenticity, it does not inherently prevent replay attacks.

Reporting (DMARC Reporting):
The mechanism by which DMARC sends aggregate and forensic reports to domain owners, providing insight into authentication results and potential abuse of the domain.

Return-Path (Envelope From):
The email header field used during SMTP transmission to indicate where bounces and delivery notifications should be sent. Aligning the Return-Path domain with SPF and DKIM helps achieve DMARC alignment.

S

Selector (DKIM Selector):
A label used to locate the public key in DNS for verifying a DKIM signature. Multiple selectors allow for easy key rotation and management.

Sender Policy Framework (SPF):
An email authentication protocol that specifies which servers are authorized to send emails on behalf of a domain, reducing spoofing and improving trust.

Social Engineering:
A set of tactics that exploit human psychology to trick individuals into divulging confidential information or performing actions against their interests.

Spam:
Unsolicited bulk emails that clutter inboxes and can serve as vectors for phishing, malware, or fraud.

Spoofing:
The act of forging email headers to make a message appear as if it originated from a trusted source, commonly used in phishing and BEC attacks.

T

TLS-RPT (Transport Layer Security Reporting):
A mechanism that provides reports on email transmission issues encountered when using MTA-STS for encrypted email delivery. It helps administrators identify and fix encryption-related problems.

Transport Layer Security (TLS):
A cryptographic protocol that ensures privacy between communicating applications. In email, TLS encrypts the connection between mail servers, preventing eavesdropping and tampering.

Trustworthiness (Email):
The perception that an email and its sender are genuine, reliable, and not attempting to deceive or harm the recipient. Achieved through consistent authentication and adherence to security best practices.

Two-Factor Authentication (2FA):
A type of MFA requiring users to provide two forms of identification (e.g., a password and a code from a mobile app) for enhanced account security.

U

Unauthorized Sender:
An email sender not listed or authorized in SPF or DKIM records and not passing DMARC, potentially indicating a spoofed or malicious source.

Z

Zero Trust Model:
A security framework that assumes no user or device, inside or outside the network, should be trusted by default. Every email and request is continuously verified to prevent unauthorized access and reduce risk.

Resource List

Official Documentation & Standards

IETF (Internet Engineering Task Force):
- **SPF Specification**: RFC 7208 - https://www.rfc-editor.org/rfc/rfc7208
- **DKIM Specification:** RFC 6376 - https://www.rfc-editor.org/rfc/rfc6376
- **DMARC Specification:** RFC 7489 - https://www.rfc-editor.org/rfc/rfc7489

BIMI Working Group: https://bimigroup.org/
MTA-STS and TLS-RPT Specifications:
- **MTA-STS:** RFC 8461 - https://www.rfc-editor.org/rfc/rfc8461
- **TLS Reporting:** RFC 8460 - https://www.rfc-editor.org/rfc/rfc8460

Diagnostic and Testing Tools

- **MXToolbox:** https://mxtoolbox.com/

Test DNS records, SPF, DKIM, and DMARC configurations and identify potential issues.

- **Mail-Tester:** https://www.mail-tester.com/

Check spam score and verify authentication for sample emails.

- **Google Postmaster Tools:** https://postmaster.google.com/

Gain insights into email deliverability, spam rates, and authentication performance for messages sent to Gmail users.

- **DMARCian:** https://dmarcian.com/

Analyze DMARC reports, visualize sending sources, and gain insights on improving authentication.

Email Security Training & Awareness

- **Phishing Simulation Platforms (e.g., KnowBe4, PhishMe):**

Conduct simulated phishing campaigns, track user responses, and provide training modules to improve employee vigilance.

- **SANS Security Awareness Training:** https://www.sans.org/security-awareness-training/

Comprehensive cybersecurity awareness resources, including email-focused materials.

- **US-CERT (Cybersecurity & Infrastructure Security Agency):** https://www.cisa.gov/

Guidance and best practices on phishing defense and email security recommended by a U.S. government agency.

Industry Insights and Threat Intelligence

- **Anti-Phishing Working Group (APWG):** https://apwg.org/

Research, data, and best practices for combating phishing and online fraud.

- **Spamhaus:** https://www.spamhaus.org/

Blocklists, threat intelligence, and resources to help identify and prevent malicious email sending domains.

- **VirusTotal:** https://www.virustotal.com/

Analyze suspicious files and URLs to detect malware, trojans, and other threats in email attachments.

DNS Management & Hosting

- **Cloudflare:** https://www.cloudflare.com/

Provides reliable DNS with built-in security features, useful for maintaining SPF, DKIM, and DMARC records.

- **AWS Route 53:** https://aws.amazon.com/route53/

A scalable and highly available DNS service that simplifies managing DNS records for email authentication.

- **GoDaddy DNS Management:** https://www.godaddy.com/

Common DNS provider with straightforward tools to publish authentication records.

Email Encryption & Secure Transmission

- **Let's Encrypt:** https://letsencrypt.org/

A free, automated, and open Certificate Authority providing TLS certificates, essential for securing SMTP connections.

- **OpenSSL:** https://www.openssl.org/

Open-source tools and libraries to generate and manage encryption keys and certificates.

Cloud-Based Email Security Providers:

- **Microsoft Defender for Office 365:** https://learn.microsoft.com/en-us/defender-office-365/mdo-about

Offers AI-driven threat protection, anti-phishing, and automated response capabilities.

- **Google Workspace Security:** https://workspace.google.com/security/

Provides built-in spam, phishing, and malware defenses, along with advanced reporting and encryption features.

- **Cisco Secure Email:**
  https://www.cisco.com/site/in/en/products/security/secure-email/index.html

Enterprise-level solution that integrates threat intelligence, domain protection, and encryption.

Incident Response & Cybersecurity Best Practices

- **NIST Cybersecurity Framework:** https://www.nist.gov/cyberframework

Guidance on identifying, protecting, detecting, responding to, and recovering from cyber incidents, including email-based attacks.

- **ENISA (European Union Agency for Cybersecurity):**
  https://www.enisa.europa.eu/

Research, guidelines, and best practices for protecting against phishing, ransomware, and email threats.

www.ingramcontent.com/pod-product-compliance
Lightning Source LLC
Chambersburg PA
CBHW071102240526
45471CB00016B/2407